CANDLE THERAPY

CANDLE THERAPY

A Magical Guide to Life Enhancement

CATHERINE RIGGS-BERGESEN, PSY.D.

**Andrews McMeel
Publishing**

Kansas City

Candle Therapy: A Magical Guide to Life Enhancement

03 04 05 06 07 MLT 10 9 8 7 6 5 4 3 2 1

Library of Congress Cataloging-in-Publication Data

Riggs-Bergesen, Catherine.
 Candle therapy : a magical guide to life enhancement / Catherine Riggs-Bergesen.
 p. cm.
 ISBN: 0-7407-3855-0
 1. Candles and lights—Miscellanea. 2. Magic. I. Title.

BF1623.C26R54 2003
133.4'3—dc21

2003050304

Book design and composition by Holly Camerlinck
Illustrations rendered by Ji Thomas

Attention: Schools and Businesses

Andrews McMeel books are available at quantity discounts with bulk purchase for educational, business, or sales promotional use. For information, please write to: Special Sales Department, Andrews McMeel Publishing, 4520 Main Street, Kansas City, Missouri 64111.

In the text, the symbol for Registered Trademark is implied and will not be used next to the references to *Candle Therapy*®, in order to promote ease of reading.

Please do not leave candles unattended. Do not take any of these items internally. In matters of physical and mental health, please consult healthcare professionals. These rituals and concepts are suggestions only; results are not guaranteed. The efforts and results are yours. Good luck and blessings!

CANDLE THERAPY *is dedicated to all seekers and finders.*

CONTENTS

◆

CONTENTS

~ PART III ~
LOVE . . . 41

CONTENTS

CONTENTS

CONTENTS

There is a long history of making wishes on candles. In today's world, we do it once a year on birthdays. Candle Therapy encourages you to bring that tradition of wishing (and being special) into your everyday life. Candle burning is an ancient technique used by practitioners of all religions through the ages and is a powerful twentieth-century therapeutic technique for change. Every single day since I opened my first store (dedicated to the principles of Candle Therapy and aromatherapy), in 1993, I have seen it work. My second store, by the name of Candle Therapy, opened in 1997 to meet the demand.

The results of working with candles are often shown in startling and moving ways. Some people have gotten true love, a major movie part, or just enough money to pay this month's rent. Sometimes results are the first step in a long road or the clarity to take the other fork in the road. Other times, working with candles results in a beautiful reawakening, opening you to the simplicity, truth, and symbolic depth of things around you. It's like having the sun finally bathe your face in warmth and light after a harsh winter, or watching a slow-falling leaf be wafted up by a current of air. Daily, people visit me to report the results of their work with candles—and it's thrilling for me. It provides the kind of instant gratification you don't often get as a therapist.

I've seen it in my life, too. Since I have dedicated myself to helping on this level, my life has completely changed. My goals keep redefining themselves and doors keep opening. The obstacles along the way merely enrich the reward and my appreciation of it. It has taught me the process of living life to the fullest. Not only have I been endlessly blessed, I have been taught to see the blessings that I often raced by in my haste to the big goal, and which have been there all along.

ACKNOWLEDGMENTS

◆

Choosing the higher path is often difficult, but that path is lined with great knowledge and growth. Even though it may not feel like it at the time, we are given what we can handle and the painful lessons bring the deepest wisdom and strength.

Special thanks to Paul and all my parents who, through their love, give me the strength to keep choosing the higher path.

More thanks to Maria Szabo, Matthew G. Rosenberger, and Jesse Wilson for their warm and brilliant efforts that facilitated this book.

PART I

THE PRINCIPLES OF CANDLE THERAPY

❧ WHY CANDLES? ❧

Candles have long been associated with the granting of wishes. We still blow out candles on our birthdays. Working with Candle Therapy can bring those special moments of a birthday candle into our daily lives. The roots of our spirituality come from the awareness of, and communication with, someone or something more powerful than us. This spiritual power is a source to lead, teach, and help us make our wishes come true. The oldest ways to reach the gods have been to use fire and scent. Flame, smoke, and perfumes have form, but also are, in part, invisible. The smoke and scent molecules waft into the air, carrying a desire, thought, or prayer. They disappear as if they were slipping through some door into the heavens.

Working with candles merges our daily reality with the spiritual. It also involves balancing and working with physical things and spiritual energies. The physical act of carving transfers your energy and links you to the work. You can see, feel, and manipulate the candle's form. Your wishes are being injected into the wax as you carve. During the burning of your candle, energy is again transferred and transmuted: Physically, the wax is burned and evaporated. The physical and visible then becomes invisible and of the other world. Spiritually, your prayers are being sent to the spiritual realm.

Since energy can neither be created nor destroyed, you are changing the energy (your prayers and ideas) into concrete results on the earthly plane. The energy can change and, thereby, *cause* creation. This creation is Magic. In that same way, Candle Therapy is *creation* of your new life. With candles, you are creating a personal tool for changing your life. The first step to your new life is ritual, which will be discussed in the next sections.

~ DOES CANDLE THERAPY WORK? ~

In my experience—yes! As I mentioned earlier, it is very fulfilling for me to see people's results, often immediately. Over the years, thousands have reported repeated blessings using candles. The power of Candle Therapy and its tools, such as incense and oils, has changed people's lives or just helped them to enjoy their lives and what they have (no little feat). One woman who comes into my store described lighting the Sun incense in the morning instead of having an eye-opening cup of coffee.

~ HOW DOES IT WORK? ~

Candle Therapy is the therapeutic use of the energy of a candle to transform energy and, thus, your life. These symbols and the process of carving candles are ways of using ritual to focus one's mind on a goal and the steps to achieve it. Candle Therapy merges one's psychological goals with one's spirituality. The psychology part involves doing all you can on the earthly plane to achieve your goals. You must focus, define your aim, and take action. Then, you must gain the necessary skills and insights for your dream to come true. In addition, psychologically, candles are soothing and make you feel like you are not alone in your efforts—and you're not! You could even view this text as a series of exercises, similar to what a cognitive therapist might assign as therapeutic "homework." On a Self-Psychological level, a candle acts as a "self-object." The self-object is an object that is a reflection of self, upon which you act. The candle reflects the spiritual and ethical changes you would like to bring about in yourself. It burns as a reminder and symbol of your desire. Candle Therapy, however, differs from a psychological technique because of the essential involvement of your spirituality. Sometimes we have to hand our dreams over to a force more powerful than we are. Everything in this book is intended for the highest good and is in no way counter to any religious beliefs. All religions use candles and have their own magic.

There are no guarantees that your wishes will be fulfilled *the way you envision them*. Your goals and vision will change and clarify as the candle is burning. Additionally, you must always assess whether there are spiritual and life plans for you about which you do not know. Maybe you have not seen the final consequences of your request, because candles sometimes do not bring the results right away. You must be persistent to achieve that big goal. Acknowledge and address the steps along the way. For example, if you are trying to finalize negotiations for selling your house, burn candles for the negotiations to be smooth for each party, your lawyer to do the best for you, the bank to accept and process the mortgage rapidly, etc. Maybe you have reached only the first step of your dream. That's great! Congratulations! Now keep going.

Cynics about magic dismiss it, saying it works only if you believe. Certainly, belief is a strong element of any successful effort. Belief in something's effectiveness explains the "placebo effect." We can even regain our health through faith. But, it's not all faith; it's also a power beyond you. These techniques and methods have been used and passed down for centuries and have great power in themselves. My observations confirm that Candle Therapy works if you make the effort, whether you believe in it or not.

~ MERGING PSYCHOLOGY AND MAGIC ~

There are many psychological orientations and approaches to therapy. If you want to go down that path, they all can help. You have to choose the style that's right for you and addressing your dilemma. Psychotherapy can bring about not only insight, but also *change* in an individual . . . almost like magic.

Similarly, change is instrumental to magic. The controversial ceremonial magician from the early part of the twentieth century, Aleister Crowley, wrote that, "Magick is the science and art of causing change to occur in conformity to will." Simplistically, defining what you want and focusing upon it (and, thereby, performing Magic), causes change in you, your environment, and those with whom you interact. Similarly, Sigmund Freud studied the role of will in psychology and health. He worked with "conversion disorders" in which, without medical basis, one of his patient's hands would go numb or eyes would go blind, because of exposure to something unacceptable. He theorized that the unconscious was a powerful force in the makeup of the individual.

Important foundations of magic and psychology were laid in the early part of the twentieth century by two unaffiliated great thinkers. Although many people, then and now, criticize and misunderstand Aleister Crowley and Sigmund Freud, it is undeniable how they have changed the way we think about, respectively, magic and the world around us. Crowley's negative reputation stemmed from his flashy antics and explorations into the spirit world. Nonetheless, he contributed invaluable spiritual insights and established many of the roots of modern Western magic. Sigmund Freud was responsible for the creation of "talk" therapy and much of our framework and understanding of psychology today. In his writings, he said that he hoped that his work would be merely a jumping-off point, from which there would be great growth and innovation. Both of these astounding men stated that their foundations were to be built upon, not be the final word of truth.

Candle Therapy is a merging of magic and psychotherapy to bring about positive change. It is a step-by-step system, performing a similar function to traditional psychotherapy, but involving one's own magic. The book is written almost in a cookbook fashion, outlining steps to attain goals. It suggests ways to progressively heal relationships and promote personal growth. If you are currently in psychotherapy, this book can only enhance the process. If you are hurting, unhappy, addicted, or not living to your utmost, I also encourage you to consider finding a therapist.

~ CONTROL ISSUES AND MORE ABOUT HOW MAGIC WORKS ~

Sometimes growth and life seem to be out of your control. It may seem like life lessons have been presented in a random and overwhelming fashion. By focusing on and working through the issues with Candle Therapy, you can change the way healing and learning occurs in you. With candles, you don't have to do it all yourself, because you've sent up your prayer and you now have powerful extra help. You can feel calmer and like you have more control over your life.

But part of control is relinquishing it. Magic is not to be used to control the wills of others. Be sure to read the section ahead on Ethics, page 9. Additionally, since you are not focusing on the results, but the steps, you are employing your faith that the best will, ultimately, happen. This requires relinquishing control of what we think must happen.

Examine the far-reaching consequences of your actions. It is hard to be brutally honest with yourself. We are human and pray for certain things because we want them. There is the axiom: You don't often receive, unless you ask. *Asking is not a problem; the problem can be staying open to what is best and what the universe sends you.* It may be even better than what you had planned. With each candle, the statement that you want the highest good for all involved must accompany your request. You don't want someone to lose his or her job so you can get it. You don't want to draw money by the cashier giving you the wrong change, because they will get stuck for a short cash drawer. You don't want to force a lover to want you, because it's manipulation of someone's will, has to be renewed constantly, and you will never know if their love is true.

Two inscriptions over a doorway at the Oracle at Delphi are key to our fulfillment today: Know thyself and practice all things in moderation.

∾ THE PROCESS ∾

In America, we are used to the quick fix, even in religion and therapy. In the same way, magical spells receive a lot of media attention. The idea of getting what we want (and we want it now!) is flashy and entertaining. Spells have been depicted as a way of getting anything, just by rubbing a genie's bottle or twitching your nose.

Candle Therapy isn't spells; it's steps. Magical and psychological workings involve *process*. Think about the expression, "sit for a spell." A spell is a part of time—a process.

We have become used to cure-alls, taking pills, and desperately trying to avoid pain, often at the cost of causing it. Pain is a necessary signal of something wrong or something to which you must attend. Although the process of achievement may sometimes be unpleasant or lengthy, it is necessary for growth. For example, if you got married without the process of spending time with your partner, you would not know the person you were marrying. Therefore, you would not have shared the experiences and little in-jokes that make a relationship gratifying. Time can further deepen love and enrich trust. You may even discover that this may not be your perfect mate!

We gain our depth and enjoyment from the process of achieving who we are. You might not believe me. You might be saying that you want to be rich, famous, married, pregnant, or the president *now*! But, think of what would happen if you achieved your final goal now. Are you ready? Truly ready? What would you miss experiencing? Would you really enjoy it? Or would it feel empty, since you didn't go through the process to achieve it for real? You may still not believe me, but read on.

The therapeutic principle underlying Candle Therapy can be called "Process Therapy." The term "Process Therapy" may seem redundant, because, obviously, therapy is a process. The term is meant to emphasize the curative importance of your participation in the process. If you are merely informed about how to solve your problems, there is no emotional discovery linked to it. Without emotional discoveries, there can be no growth and, thereby, no process.

THE KEYS TO THE PROCESS

The fulfillment of life is a process. The basis of our growth revolves around goals and dreams in this process. One reaches a goal. Then, one sets another. The experiences along the way make us who we are. This is the real magic.

DEFINE YOUR GOALS

Books about magic tend to emphasize goals. "Get this," "do this," and "achieve this" are all very action-oriented ideas. Goals involving one's success, love, finance, health, luck, and self-growth are a constant part of life.

Even Candle Therapy is goal-oriented. But with Candle Therapy, the goal is not the ruling aspect of the magic. We need a goal to organize our thoughts. The secret is to be open to the journey to your goal and trust that you will be given what is best for you.

The first step is to define and clarify your goals. Make lists or use whatever method necessary for your clarity. Explore how to reach the goal and assess what steps are involved. Defining your psychological goals has a practical side. You will know what you have to do in the real world to get something achieved.

In order for Candle Therapy to work, you must put forth a practical effort too. You cannot stop looking for work because you are sure you are going to win the lottery. You must make those phone calls and do what you can on the earthly plane to realize your dream. Develop your skills so that when the opportunity comes, you will be ready.

After you define your desire and burn a candle, assess the results and progress to the next level with your goal. In this way you can gain a deeper level of psychological health and regain control of your life. This book will suggest the next candle to burn on your path to success, love, healing, recovery, and growth. It even offers alternative paths if your results are different from what you envisioned.

SET REASONABLE GOALS

Research has shown, repeatedly, that those who are depressed tend to set unreasonable goals for themselves. One technique to remedy depression is to help the person learn to set reachable goals. This assures that he or she receives reinforcement along the way. Then they can keep going.

ENJOY THE PROCESS

As stated previously, Candle Therapy is based on the *process* of magic. One cannot always achieve the final goal by burning one candle. For example, if you want to become famous, there are steps you must take before getting there. You must develop skill and confidence, be able to attract an audience, practice, learn, make connections, and develop yourself so that who you are becomes part of your creative expression. If you want to find love, you may have to take steps to let go of your past loves and hurts, as well as becoming more open to new love. This new openness may involve going to more parties, accepting blind dates, and flirting. Learning to enjoy the process of growing into the best you can be is enriching. Again, the process makes you stronger.

If you reach your goal too early, it will be terrifying. You may not be ready or you may not appreciate it as much as if you worked as hard as you could to get there. If you aren't good enough to stay on your perch, you will not keep your goal for long. In essence, without the process, we cannot enjoy the end result.

❧ THE IMPORTANCE AND PHYSIOLOGY OF RITUAL ❧

Fundamentally, rituals are preparations that alter your state of mind and lend greater significance and focus to a tool or event. Certainly, prayers and signs that we do in front of an altar are rituals. Nonetheless, not all rituals are strictly spiRITUAL in nature. All of us perform hundreds of them daily. The practical tasks of putting on makeup or shaving signal you that it's time for work. These rituals shift your state of being from sleepy to focused. On your day off, sitting around in your robe and sleeping late signals you to relax and forget your weekly focus. Even buying a new piece of clothing for a special occasion is a ritual. This makes the event more meaningful to you. Your goal may be to feel a certain way in the clothing—more powerful, more beautiful, sexy, or more fun.

Once you are aware of the rituals in your life, you will see what powerful tools they are for the enhancement of your life. Overall, rituals touch us mentally and physically. They are vital, on many levels, to our healing, growth, and spiritual experience. Rituals such as marriages and funerals intensify and focus important passages. Many people argue against having props, such as candles, of any kind. They feel that if they were truly enlightened or in touch with their spirituality, they "shouldn't" need props. They believe they "should" be able to manifest and alter their state without any help. Part of spirituality is realizing we are in a human form and do need help. Even "transcended masters" are human and use props. Although the transcended masters may not *need* rituals or props to induce a spiritual state, I am sure they would wonder—Why not? Why not use ritual? It is a beautiful enrichment of our lives.

A candle is a wonderful ritual tool. It is merely wax until you transform it into a concrete manifestation of your prayer. The ritual of transforming (or "dressing") a magical candle calls upon your mental and physical skills. Mentally, you must call upon your will, focus, and intent. Physically, all your senses are involved. With practice you will find that the most powerful rituals you perform will not only be mental exercises, but be paired with sensory experience. Preparing a candle involves all your senses.

AROMATHERAPY

Smell is one of the most important senses involved in preparing candles. Sensory information, with the exception of olfactory input, is transmitted to the brain's cortex for higher-level processing via a central switching station called the thalamus. Olfactory input, however, is relayed directly to the most primitive part of the brain, the limbic system. The limbic system, found in all primates, is the seat of many things, including emotion, memory, and sexuality. Research has even demonstrated the link between these structures and spirituality. As shocking as it may seem, spirituality can be surgically induced! As cited in the June 24, 1996, issue of *Time* magazine, electronic stimulation of the amygdala or the hippocampus during surgery can bring on visions of angels and devils. Because of its link to the limbic system, smell can evoke deep emotions, sexuality, memories, and spirituality. As examples:

- For relaxation, happiness, and motivation, some factories in Japan have propelled a blend of lavender and peppermint through the vents.
- For sexual attraction, many perfume companies add the attraction tool of animals—musk. Because of laws protecting animals, these musks are now synthetic, but molecularly similar to animal pheromones.
- Memory can be evoked by smelling something that you have not smelled since the time the original memory was created. This can inspire positive or negative responses within you. Companies that use vanilla or cinnamon in their products certainly hope you have positive experiences with baked goods and the secure memories they can trigger.

Dressing a candle can evoke emotions, sexual feelings, and memories; it also binds the power of smell to spirituality. Smelling the oils and incenses can bring about a spiritual state. The sense of smell is linked to taste due to similar structural and neural pathways through the hypothalamus. For example, drinking damiana tea can produce aphrodisiac effects, which can also be felt if the herb is burned or is part of an incense blend. A listing of oils and their purposes can be found in the Appendix.

TASTE

Magical undertakings always involve an offering. The offering is a symbol that in order to receive, you are willing to give. The offering can take many forms. Some people do a good deed. Some drop coins or flower petals in the bottom of the candle glass (if you are using a "seven-day candle" in a glass jar). Some make offerings with honey.

Tasting the honey and/or coating the bottom of a candle glass with honey is a very appropriate offering for your magical candle work. Physically, the ritual of tasting honey involves the hypothalamus's function of mediating hunger and satiety. The honey also signals a feeling of comfort and fulfillment.

SOUND

Sound can have a physical effect as well. Making a very loud sound (90–100 decibel range) can double the amount of blood pumped, per second, through a heart. In the Chinese "Feast of the Hungry Ghosts," metal plates and pans are clanged to scare away the evil ghosts. Hearing your prayer or desire spoken aloud or any accompanying music can bring you into a more spiritual state. You might prefer using a bell. Its pure sound can turn the mundane into a lofty experience. The physical aspects of sound are delineated in Harvard Medical School's "Spirituality and Healing in Medicine II" course description. It states that by engaging in a "repetitive prayer, word, sound, or phrase," stress levels can be reduced, effectively treating symptoms of hypertension, pain, insomnia, infertility, cancer, AIDS, PMS, mild anxiety, and depression.

TOUCH

Holding the candle, while you contemplate your task and carve the seals, involves the sense of touch. Touching floods your brain's parietal lobe with messages. Applying the oils to the candle further enhances this tactile experience.

SIGHT

Candle Therapy is also visual. The symbols of Candle Therapy may seem familiar, as if you have seen some of them (in sum or in part) before. You may feel attracted to some of them. These ancient symbols have been used for so many centuries; they are a solid part of the huge pool of human thought, symbols, and values that has persisted through the ages. We may inherently know and feel the depth of these symbols without being taught.

❧ ETHICS ❧

Ethics are one of the most important aspects of Candle Therapy.

Burning candles is about ethics, healing, and change. Always try to think of a way to achieve your goal in the most healing, ethical, and positive way. Magical transformation, itself, is neither good nor bad. What you do with it determines whether it is black, white, or gray magic. Your intentions make a candle good or evil.

Every religion has its magic, using tools of candles, oils, incense, and prayer. So this is just furthering whatever your spiritual beliefs are. Nothing you do with Candle Therapy is counter to your religious framework. It is an enhancement of yourself and your beliefs.

Examine your everyday ethics. Do you consider yourself to be ethical and dedicated to good? *Choices to be honest keep your mind clear for more essential functions.* Sometimes, we might do things in an easy way, instead of an ethical way. But every unethical choice you make hangs on you like a little dark badge on your knit sweater. The sweater ultimately gets very heavy and very dark, and needs a good wash. You become very unhappy and things aren't going right. Maybe your sweater even smells and repulses your lover. Now you're in a fine mess, and it started with small things and metaphysically accumulated blackness. This blackness is a burden, weighing you down.

Freedom consists of always choosing the higher path. This means not lying, cheating, stealing, or maliciously hurting another. This may seem easy when read, but examine the little fibs or cheats of your day. Sometimes we fib out of insecurity and fear of consequences. The consequences usually are not as bad as we fear. If they are, we may need to take responsibility and not create false realities for ourselves and others. It can be hard at first, but ultimately, it is liberating and builds confidence.

Manipulation of others should be avoided at all costs. It does not work. And if it does, it won't be long before it will have bad effects. Be aware of your agenda. All Candle Therapy should be performed with a desire for the highest good of everyone involved. If you are not sure your intentions are pure, say your wish aloud and add, "for the highest good of everyone involved"—and mean it.

One purpose of candles is to enhance what is already happening. For example, love candles should accentuate and develop what is already occurring. *Do not manipulate or force another to be in love with you—even if you determine it is fate for you to be together!* Let things go their natural way. Building trust in the other person might require patience on your part. Rushing it could kill the relationship. If it's all taking too long, you might want to examine whether this relationship is in your best interest.

In addition, having someone against their will (by enchantment) is like not having them at all. The magic must be renewed constantly, and you will never be sure if it is your magic or true love operating. *Whatever you do magically comes back to you three times.* This is called The Law of Three and operates in all magic. If you want someone to love you, they will by your enchantment, but *you* will become *three times more in love with them.* Also—they may be in love, but not know why. Since they have no shared experiences with you to justify the intensity of their flame (created by your magic), their logic will tell them to *run!*

Do not hex, cross, or be vengeful to others, no matter how tempted. If you have been hurt and want to bring justice to that person (what you determine is justice), take a long look before you leap. Your spirit of revenge and punishment of another will bring three times the hurt back to your doorstep. The boss who fired you will only hate you more if you seek revenge. Try to heal the situation so that when the boss thinks of you, he or she will think fondly of you. Throw a little healing your way, too, to reduce your bitterness. Feelings of revenge will eat you up, make you sick, unhappy, and continue a destructive circle. If you have been "cursed," read the section on Clearing, Protection, and Justice, page 181. If you involve yourself in wanting a person to "get a dose of their own medicine," you will suffer three times more than they will. *There are no exceptions.* And very importantly, *you will continue to be linked to them.* They hurt you, you hurt them back, your bad wishes come back on you, on and on—and it does not end. In this manner, they cannot get out of your life and you cannot win. Wishing them evil can only bind you together until you stop the chain and protect yourself from the person permanently. Faith in "what goes around comes around" will keep your life progressing and free.

The higher path is to trust, *strongly,* that if there has been a genuine wrong done to you or your loved ones, the perpetrator will pay. The "laws of karma" will punish this person in far more horrendous ways than you can envision or wish upon them. So keep your energy out of the circle.

The higher path is often hard to choose. It is hard to climb.
This path will keep you winning, although it may not seem like it during the trek.

~ BOTTOM LINE ~

~ *As you do your candles and ask for things, not only will you get what you ask for, but also your desire will be redefined.* You will become focused through the ritual of doing the candles. You will also get a clear ethical vision and awareness of the consequences of your acts. You have to know, reasonably, what goals you can reach. Once you gain a sense of control through doing your candles (in conjunction with your spirituality), you will have an important tool. Candle Therapy will be a lifelong tool that will help you learn to live optimally.

~ *A candle sends out your hopes and requests for as long as it burns—and longer.* This frees you to live without obsession and grants a feeling that you have handed your problem over to a much more powerful force than yourself. One could wonder why a god/goddess or spirit guides do not automatically see what has to be done and do it. Candles are often a way for your higher force to urge you to get back in touch with your spirituality. Also, we often do not receive unless we focus and ask. But again, be clear and specific in what you request.

~ *Remember that you get what you pray for!* Always think of the consequences of your request. Is it against someone's will? Were you specific? Are you truly open to how the answer will come? There is an old tale about a medieval family who got three wishes. They used the first wish for money. There was a knock on the door. A messenger from the King sent them more riches than they could imagine. The accompanying note explained that the King was very sorry for killing their son in a hunting accident and hoped the money would compensate. Stricken with grief, the family used the remaining wishes to erase the first wish. The next knock on the door was the son returning from his journey in the woods—alive. The money disappeared.

Whatever you do comes back to you three times. Whatever you do should be for the highest good of all concerned. Always thank whomever you believe in and whoever helps you spiritually. So, do good candles and good acts and be happy.

◆

PART II

PREPARATION FOR
CARVING

David Schulhoff

∿ A QUICK GUIDE TO
CANDLE PREPARATION ∿

The following is a brief summary of the tools for and steps of preparing a magical candle. Each one of the steps will be elucidated in the following sections. This list of steps is handy when you need a reference outlining the steps. *One tool that is not necessary is artistic ability.* The process of copying the symbol, however it looks at the end, is the goal. The effort and concentration are also the magic.

STEPS

1. *Assess your purpose,* keeping in mind what is best for everyone involved. For this you need will, motivation, and openness.
2. *Purify and prepare* for the focus and spiritual work ahead.
3. *Choose:*
   A. The kind of *candle.*

B.   The *color* of the candle..

C.   One or two *seals* from this book, addressing the aspects of your purpose.

D.   One or two *oils*, also addressing aspects of your wish (one for the wick and the other for the candle's surface).

E.   Optionally, the *kind of incense*. Light it whenever you would like. Many burn incense to calm and center themselves and to create an atmosphere of their desire in the room.

F.   Optionally, the *color of glitter*. The glitter on the surface of the candle can help in reinforcing the symbols visually. It also can bring in the energies of the colors used.

4.   *Plan an offering.* There are many choices. You can make a symbolic offering by privately tasting honey. Alternatively, you can do something nice for someone as thanks for your blessings (even before they arrive).

5.   *Carve the seal on the candle,* carefully, with something pointy, such as an X-Acto knife, nail, fondue stick, sharp knife, or ice pick.

6.   *Anoint the candle with oil* while envisioning your request. At this point you could use glitter to outline the symbols or just sprinkle it over the candle for a beautiful glow.

7.   *Light incense.* This is an optional step you can do to help focus and create an atmosphere around you and your candle.

8.   *Glitter the seal.* This optional step makes the candle look even more special. It further ritualizes the process, thus setting the work deeper into your subconscious.

9.   *Make wishes.* Drop pennies into the candle glass and make wishes on each one. Or if you do not have a candle jar, write down your wishes and concentrate on each one for the highest good. Carry this list or place it next to the candle away from the flame or melting wax. You can review and add to the list each time you light the candle.

10.   *Burn the candle.* There are many approaches to burning a candle. I prefer burning it little by little. Each time you light it, you are renewing its energy through your attention. When you put it out, either through blowing or snuffing (your preference), say "thank you" even if the results are not yet clear. Burn all candles to the end. Not only is it respectful, but your purposes and future blessings change as the candle progresses.

11.   *Light a candle for thanks.* Pause and say "thank you" for the blessings given (even if only the first step) and for what you have.

~ ASSESS YOUR PURPOSE ~

One of the most important steps is defining your goals. What do you want and how can you accomplish it for the highest good of all involved?

Keeping in mind the section on Ethics, page 9, actively assess your desire. Are you thinking of having a zombie–love slave instead of a full, rich, give-and-take relationship that involves the building of trust through a series of experiences and joy—not blind obedience to you? Do you want to doom your boss, landlord, or new love interest of your ex-love to a horrible fate? Instead, let go and trust that everything will work out for the best. Divorce yourself from negative feelings, revenge, and asserting control over others (even in a "loving" way). You will feel free and happy.

Next, assess your purpose psychologically. Focus on what you want and be honest with yourself. Then, when you choose the seals you will carve on the candle, consider each aspect of your wish. Use one or two symbols to capture the overall concept. If there are other elements in the mix, address those through your oil or incense choice. For example, if you want to meet a perfect love, but you don't feel confident or attractive, use the seal to meet the highest love and combine it with Fearlessness and Confidence incense and Irresistibility oil. The next steps prepare you on a spiritual plane.

Now, examine your desire. Decide what you want to do and how to achieve it. Our will is one of our strongest tools. In the Bible's story of creation, the apple can, symbolically, be seen to represent the human's cerebral cortex. It is present only in humans, separates us from animals, and is the seat of our will. Will is at the core of all magic, and it is symbolized by fire. Through their fire, candles can express your will. Gather your will and the tools for carving your candle and proceed.

~ PURIFY AND PREPARE ~

Preparation for any magical work has inward and outward manifestations. Inwardly, preparations for your magic start at the moment you realize you have some magical work to do and alter your state of consciousness. If you can, start the day before your ritual to cleanse. Try to avoid cigarettes, drugs, and alcohol the night before and, definitely, during the ritual.

There is no need to alter your reality; your prayers will do it for you. *One of your most essential tools is clarity.*

CREATING SACRED SPACE

Even if you do not have a separate altar room (and few of us do), you can have a sacred space for your rituals. Any space will do. Use the top of your dresser or a windowsill. You can light incense to create an altar room anywhere! As it fills the corners of your room, it blesses the space and delineates a sacred territory. You can draw a spiritual symbol on the other side of a rug, which you flip over when you do meditation and spiritual work. The more you use one area, the more that area will hold your power. Your body, also, will learn that this area is a sacred space and immediately calm down to match the peace of the space.

CLEANSING YOUR SPACE

Cleansing your living space is a wonderful thing to do anytime. It banishes negativity and keeps vibrations clear. There are a number of ways to cleanse. A popular and powerful method is to "smudge." This usually involves sage, cedar, or lavender burned individually or in any combination. You can burn the leaves on charcoal blocks designed for incense use or light prewrapped bundles of sage or sage blends.

Carry a lit smudge counterclockwise around your house, envisioning all the darkness leaving. See all negativity spiral to the heavens. Move the energy out with your hands. Sweep it away. You may start to feel tingly and light yourself!

Once you feel the space is clean, walk clockwise around your space with frankincense or Sun incense. You will be able to feel the joy with your journey to the light.

CHOOSING AND CLEANSING TOOLS

Magical tools can include ritual items symbolizing the four elements: earth, salt; air, incense; water, chalice; and fire, candle. These tools do not need to be expensive or bought from a mystical emporium. Find the candles, as well as the bowls to hold the water and salt, at any store. You make them sacred.

Other tools include crystals and gifts from nature. Crystals and stones are wonderful for centering energy—but only if they are found-stones. Few realize that strip-mining is increasing to meet the heavy demand for crystals. Wands can be made from branches of willow, birch, or any wood that feels special to you. Be sure to ask the tree for permission to take a branch and leave an offering. Whenever you take from the earth, ask permission, and give thanks and offerings (more about offerings later, on page 25).

What you wear is a tool for magic, as well. It is advisable to set aside a piece of clothing that you wear only for ritual. It can be any outfit that feels clean, comfortable, and respectful.

Other tools include bells and talismans. Bells are tools that alter consciousness and help involve more of your senses. They also call spirits and gods. Talismans and charms are often images of ancient symbology that have great strength, even though they're often made in a factory-setting with no spiritual preparation. These symbols have been used for so many years (sometimes for centuries) that they have power even without your focus, as do the symbols in this book. The real power comes with your concentration and focus.

Tools can be blessed and purified similarly to a space. Pass them through pure water or smoke of a banishing or blessing incense. You can also leave a tool on a windowsill so the light of the moon or the sun purifies it. You can consecrate a tool or talisman by holding it between your palms. Focus on its purpose and how it can help you. Then, pray. Your prayer can be formal, informal, or both. You can do a formal prayer that you know from your religious background. You can also formulate your own or just speak your dreams and intentions aloud. A sample prayer would be as follows:

Dear _____ (whoever helps you spiritually),

Please
grant me the strength to achieve this (describe what you wish for)
OR
bring me a true love (describe the qualities of this person)
OR
bring me the money I so dearly need at this time to pay _____ (list debts) _____.

The *minimum* I require is _____. I would appreciate more, but would so appreciate the minimum.

Thank you with all my heart. I do not wish to manipulate or harm. I pray that my request can be granted for the highest good of all involved.

This consecration method collects your personal energy. It is there for you when you feel weak or need its innate power. Just hold the tool or talisman in your hand and concentrate on your desire.

MEDITATION

To prepare yourself for your meditation, take a purifying bath. Add a handful of sea salt, petals of a beautiful flower, or relaxing herbs such as lavender and chamomile to a tub of hot water. You can also add a dash of magical oil, prepared for your purpose. For cleansing, throw in the petals of white flowers. For love, you can also add petals of yellow, pink, or white roses.

Relax. Breathe deeply. While in the bath, concentrate upon releasing blocks and impurities. Next, concentrate upon your goal and how it can be achieved for the highest good of all involved.

Meditation and visualization are some more important tools. Your methods can be TM, progressive relaxation, self-hypnosis, and informal visualization. Meditation and focus are the keys to centering your will. Meditation also helps clarify the issues so you can be as specific as possible. In one way, working with candles is an act of faith—a way to send your prayer to a higher spirit. In another way, it's a release. Define what you want and act upon that desire by doing the candle and then stop trying to control things. Certainly, continue trying to achieve your goal on the earthly plane, but let go. Turn over some of the chore to a higher force. If you are not a believer in a higher force, then know you have done all you can do psychologically, until you receive an answer to your request.

A fabulous book called *Spells and How They Work* by Janet and Stewart Farrar delightfully outlines many examples of what happens when you are not specific in magical work. You may achieve your goal, but not in the way it was envisioned. For example, you may get Monopoly money or money in another currency. In all meditations with your candle, be specific or you may be unpleasantly surprised at the results.

Although I am encouraging you to be specific, *do not be rigid*. There are no guarantees and no assured ways your results will manifest. Each of our paths is very different. Through the power of your mind, envision the end result and let spirituality make your dreams become reality.

Important: Do not be demanding. In your meditations with the candle, always say "please" and "thank you" to whomever or whatever you believe in and guides you spiritually. Always emphasize that your magical working is merely a request—a strong request—but you understand that whatever happens will be for the highest good and may not manifest exactly as you envision it. We don't always know what is best for us. It does not hurt to ask for what you want, but try to be open: The universe may have other plans for you.

~ CHOOSE ~

THE KIND OF CANDLE

Usually, candles are made from paraffin, stearite, vegetable fats, or beeswax. Some of us have preferences based upon the ingredients, but no one kind is more spiritual than another. The bottom line is that wax is wax; it is the power with which you imbue it that makes it different. Also, the size or shape of the candle does not dictate its power, only how long it burns. Therefore, if you need more than a zap of power and your request may not happen overnight, you may need a longer-burning candle.

David Schulhoff

Any candle upon which you can carve will do.

THE COLOR OF THE CANDLE

Choosing a color with which to work is one of the most important steps in the magical process. Color, through energy, evokes emotion and an altered state. Color is light and light is energy. The work of a candle is moving energy and translating energy into will—and therefore performing magic.

Color	Meaning
White or Silver	White is the presence and balance of all colors. You can transform a white candle into any color, spiritually; just imbue it with that vibration. It is used for protection, clearing, healing, meditation, purification, light, and blessing. White is good for all passages, birth through death, as well as devotionals to the moon. Gets rid of negativity.
Yellow or Gold	Happiness, joy, renewal, recognition, vitality, mental power, power, vitality, will, and uncovering what is hidden. Light and encouragement of the sun. Good for bringing a soul mate kind of love, because the love that is attracted is based on friendship and joy. Out of joy often comes romance.

Color	Meaning
Orange	Success, especially in tasks of communication and writing. Adaptability, encouragement, and attraction of business and opportunities. Open doors and smooth business dealings. Use orange to gain concentration, vitality, health, and dynamic force.
Green	Money drawing, growth, healing of a woman- or growth-oriented medical issue. Good for attracting love, money, plenty, or success. Fertility, healing, abundance, attraction and/or deepening of love.
Pink	For love relationships, honor, affection, romance, and friendly feelings. More stable for love than red. Also see yellow for attracting true love.
Red	Red is about passion—passion for anything. It's for invoking lusty, powerful, and passionate energy or love. Red is a little dangerous. It's great for initiations, but whatever you are working on could *burn out* as rapidly as it started. It also can spur angry feelings. But this is *great* if you are already involved and want to stimulate lust or want to get going on a project. Excellent for fearlessness, energy, courage, strength, and skill in battles (of whatever nature).
Blue	Protection, peace, calm, tranquillity, soothing, deep justice, blessings, anger-reduction, and inspiration.
Purple	Draws in the highest divinity. Good for altar candles and devotionals (along with white). Also good for business success and expansion, joviality, generosity, and luck in court cases.
Brown	Grounding, stability, security, solidity, laws of karma, earth and material plane, justice, integrity, finalization, completion, and wisdom.
Black	When you are feeling your lowest or blackest, use black to eliminate all negativity. Channel all negativity into the black candle as it burns. Then, throw what is left far away from your house. Since black absorbs approximately 98 percent of available light, a black candle does not emit vibrations; it absorbs. Think of coming into the light, out of the blackness. Some people are scared of black, because others use it for malefic purposes. If you feel tempted to use a candle for negative motivations, remember the magical law of doing no harm and use white instead. In addition, keep in mind that whatever you do will come back to you three times (even if you can justify that the person serves" some sort of retribution).

It is also important to consider the colors of the chakras in your magical, health-oriented work. Your Chi and Kundalini power, which travels up your spine and electrifies each chakra, can be instrumental in balancing the body and providing health.

Each chakra corresponds with a color as listed below:

Chakra	Parts of the Body	Color	Chakra Number
Root	perineum, base of spine	red	1
Fifth lumbar	sacrum, genitals	orange	2
Solar plexus	below the diaphragm, behind the stomach	yellow	3
Heart	thymus, center of the chest	green	4
Throat	thyroid, base of the throat	blue	5
Third eye	pineal, brow, third eye	indigo	6
Crown of head	pituitary, top of head	violet	7

SEALS AND SYMBOLS

Seals and symbols of our goals, hopes, and dreams have been used through the ages. It has been found that even without the written word, symbols have been used, universally, to preserve and convey knowledge. According to Jung, these symbols are expressions of our longings, values, and deep truths. They are preserved within every human being and are present at birth. We inherently know and feel the depth of these symbols without being taught. Therefore, every person has access to the Collective Unconscious—the storehouse of the symbols of the ages. You will notice that many of the symbols listed below are Egyptian in origin. This just happens to be my interest and origination. In that way, this book is a minute sampling of the symbols throughout the world.

The symbols in *Candle Therapy* are a combination of ancient symbols, adaptations of traditional seals, and symbols of the Collective Unconscious. The descriptions below are a brief guide to the history and sources of the forms you will see in this book.

We all have different symbols. You may find that you cannot decide which symbols to use. Choose different ones for each aspect of the question. Try to hone it down to the minimum. Usually one or two symbols will do it. Don't choose the same idea over and over; that doesn't make it stronger.

The seals that are used in this book are suggestions. Use whatever symbols are appropriate to your needs. Also, if you do not execute the drawing of the symbols with the skills of a graphic artist, all is not lost. *Your focus, intention, and sense of respect are important—not how visually "correct" or "beautiful" your artwork is.* It is desirable to try to make it a beautiful creation in honor of your god, goddess, or yourself, but this is not the time to worry about perfection, just balance. The worry will prevent you from fully expressing your spiritual goals.

OILS

Oils can be worn, poured into a luscious bath, or used to anoint candles. They are blended during proper astrological and moon phases for these purposes. Try to use only essential or high-quality fragrance oils and the finest herbs to create magical formulae. The oils below and on page 23 are based on both ancient formulae and planetary and spiritual correspondences. Many of the oils have been used for so many centuries that you do not even have to concentrate to achieve your goals. Of course, focus and clarity are two of the most powerful magical tools. Intensify the oil with your energy and desire.

Many fine herbal and magical stores throughout the country supply oils and incenses. Many people have similar blends with different names. If it is for the right purpose and smells right to you, you probably are in tune with the blend. Don't worry about the exact name. Each part of this book has a list of oils pertinent to each purpose (love, success, protection, etc.). For a complete list of oils, please consult the Oil Appendix on page 204. From that list, you can find a blend for your purpose. You may also combine essential oils to form your personalized formulae.

As a guideline, here is a summary of suggestions:

SCENTS AND THEIR PURPOSES	
Purpose	Recommended Scents or Blends
Courage	Cedar, Frankincense, Musk, and Rose Geranium
Courage to speak	Anoint your throat with a touch of Frankincense and High John
Fertility	Musk, Vervain
Happiness	Apple, Carnation, Frankincense, and Tuberose
Harmony	Basil, Gardenia, Lilac, and Narcissus
Healing	Carnation, Coconut, Eucalyptus, Gardenia, Lotus, Myrrh, Narcissus, Rosemary, Sandalwood, and Violet
Love	Bay, Clove, Frangipani, Gardenia, Ginger, Jasmine, Lavender, Orris, Rose, Vetivert, and Violet
Luck	Cinnamon, Cypress, Lotus, and Tonka
Mind power and concentration	Honeysuckle, Lilac, and Rosemary

Purpose	Recommended Scents or Blends
Money	Almond, Basil, Bayberry, Bergamot, Cinnamon, Frankincense, Honeysuckle, Mint, Neroli, Orange, Patchouli, Pine, Tonka, and Vervain
Peace	Benzoin, Gardenia, Hyacinth, Magnolia, Rose, and Tuberose
Protection	Cypress, Myrrh, Patchouli, Rose Geranium, Rosemary, Rue, Violet, and Wisteria
Psychic awareness	Acacia, Anise, Heliotrope, Lemongrass, Lilac, Mimosa, Nutmeg, and Sandalwood
Rejuvenation	Allspice, Carnation, Eucalyptus, Rosemary, and Vanilla
Sexuality	Ambergris, Cinnamon, Civet, Clove, Musk, Patchouli, and Vanilla
Success	Allspice, Carnation, Frankincense, Rosemary, and Vanilla

INCENSES

Incenses can be an offering to whoever helps you spiritually or act as an enhancement of your request. Choose an incense specific to your purpose. It can be bought or prepared in the forms of stick, cone, or powder. Powdered incense combines herbs, oils, and wood base (so it burns). You can burn it with or without a charcoal:

Without charcoal: If it has a lot of wood base or is not too full of herbs, you can burn it right in an ashtray—it lights right up. Just put in a spoonful, light it, blow on it (carefully!), and then blow it out. A spoonful usually fills a space with a luscious smell. Relight what does not burn completely.

If you are burning a lot of powder, or resins such as frankincense, myrrh, or benzoin, use charcoal designed for incense burning (in a metal burner only!). The use of charcoal assures that all your incense will be burned, but it gives off smoke and a smell of its own.

Here is a brief guideline to incense:

INCENSES AND THEIR PURPOSES	
Purpose	Name of Incense *Names may vary with manufacturer*
Banishing spirits and ghosts	Banishing

Purpose	Name of Incense
Banishing negativity	Uncrossing
Blessing	Blessing, Isis, and Moon
Confidence	Kindly Spirit, Fearlessness, and Confidence
Courage	Frankincense and Mars, Motivation, and Sun
Calming	Chamomile, Stress Reduction, and Pax/Peace/Osiris
Energy, renewing	Carnation, Rosemary, Sun, and Vanilla
Good fortune and wealth	Frankincense, Jupiter, Mercury, Money Drawing, Success Blast, Sun, Super Fast Luck, and Venus
Grounding	Earth; Peace, Protection, and Blessings; and Saturn
Happiness	Bliss, Joy and Contentment, and Sun
House blessing	Copal; Cucumber; Frankincense; Egyptian Temple; House Blessing; Peace, Protection and Blessings; and Thyme
House cleansing	Banishing, Lavender, Lemon, Pine, Sage, and Uncrossing
Knowledge of mysteries	Clarity, High Priestess, Isis, and Mystic Seeker
Letting go and healing	Grieving and Comfort, Healing, Kyphi, and Letting Go
Love	Attract Soul mate Romance, Long-Lasting Love, Rose, and Venus
Marriage	Attract Soul mate Romance, Gardenia, and Long-Lasting Love
Overcoming obstacles	Conquering Glory, Crown of Success, and Success Blast
Prophetic visions/dreams	Flying, Moon, and Mystic Seeker
Prosperity	Bountiful Prosperity, and Success
Protection	Benzoin; Copal; Dragon's Blood; Fiery Wall of Protection; Peace, Protection, and Blessings; and Strong Protection

Purpose	Name of Incense
Restful sleep	Egyptian Temple; Lavender; Neroli; and Peace, Protection, and Blessings
Sexuality	Aphrodisiac Blend, Spiritual Sex, and Voodoo Nights Sex
Strength	Fearlessness and Confidence, Seven African Powers
Success	Amber, Arabka Soudagar, Jupiter, Money Drawing, San Ramon, Shi Shi, and Success
Uncrossing	Seven African Powers, and Uncrossing
Worship	There are too many individual gods and goddesses to list. Buy or make incense according to your personal pantheon and worshipping preference.

GLITTER

It is not always necessary to apply glitter to the candle's surface. Some people apply only oil to the surface of their candles. The glittering, however, helps to intensify the ritual and specialness of your candle. Some people rub the colored powdered incense onto the surface of the candles in order to outline the seals. Glitter serves both spiritual and psychological purposes:

1. It outlines the seal so you can see it more clearly when you meditate on your candle. It also serves to place the seal more completely into your subconscious.
2. It can make the process and candle feel more special.
3. The color of the glitter should correspond to the purposes intended (i.e., orange for communication, blue for calming, etc. See the color chart on page 19 for more specific information). Glitter can more completely attune the candle to its magical purpose. It can also attune you in your meditations to the specific aspects of your overall desires.

~ PLAN AN OFFERING; ONE MUST GIVE IN ORDER TO RECEIVE ~

Symbolic gestures of your willingness to give in order to receive are offerings. Offerings can take many forms. In candle preparation, many people use the offering of honey. Squeeze a little honey onto your left hand and taste it. Then put some honey into your candle jar or holder, if you have one. You are making a symbolic offering to Venus, derived from the legend that Venus was poisoned by honey. By tasting the honey, you are offering yourself to Venus as the taster to protect her. In essence, you are willing to give in order to receive.

Offerings must mean something to you. They do not have to be expensive, just thought-out. Every time you do a candle, give to a charity, or volunteer for a day. Make your offering without having an idea of what you will get in exchange for your kind acts. You will be blessed; you don't need to think about it.

Consider what is a suitable gift to whoever helps you spiritually. It could be flowers, coins, coconuts, shells, or a special piece of jewelry. If you take a seashell, leave an offering to the sea. You can choose a flower especially for the sea and throw the petals into the water.

~ CARVE THE SEAL ~

Hold the candle in the palm of the hand opposite from your dominant hand. (If you are left-handed, hold it in your right.) Take a knife and carve the symbols you have chosen into the wax. You can also use a pointy fondue stick, nail, or pin. If you are going to add glitter to the candle, you do not have to carve deeply into the wax. Your carving will merely act as a guideline for you to follow. If you are not using glitter, feel free to carve deeply and put your energy into the wax with every cut.

David Schulhoff

Concentrate on your intention, not the appearance of your drawing. It may be hard to free yourself from positive or negative judgments of your drawing. It is the process of carving, not the way it looks, that is important.

Also draw the first names and astrological signs of the people who will receive the blessing of the candle. If you are trying to uncross or get rid of someone, do not put his or her name on the candle. If you do not know the sign, leave it out and just inscribe the appropriate name. The following are the "glyphs" or shorthand symbols for the zodiacal signs:

ZODIAC SIGNS AND DATES					
(Mar. 21–Apr. 20)	Aries	♈	Libra	♎	(Sep. 23–Oct. 22)
(Apr. 21–May 20)	Taurus	♉	Scorpio	♏	(Oct. 23–Nov. 22)
(May 21–June 21)	Gemini	♊	Sagittarius	♐	(Nov. 23–Dec. 21)
(June 22–July 22)	Cancer	♋	Capricorn	♑	(Dec. 22–Jan. 19)
(July 23–Aug. 22)	Leo	♌	Aquarius	♒	(Jan. 20–Feb. 18)
(Aug. 23–Sep. 22)	Virgo	♍	Pisces	♓	(Feb. 19–Mar. 20)

~ APPLY OIL ~

The purpose of applying oil to the surface of a candle is twofold: to intensify the purpose and to make the glitter stick to the candle's surface.

After choosing an oil, pour a small amount in the center of your cupped palm. It's a good idea to wear latex gloves because extensive exposure to oils may cause an allergic reaction, and some oils are naturally irritating. If you carve with your right hand, pour the oil into your left palm and vice versa if you are left-handed.

Smear the oil up and down the candle. Some people prefer to apply oil in a set pattern. The usual pattern is to apply the oil to the center of the candle, smear it upward, and then downward. This is to acknowledge that our prayers are sent upward and then come down to the earthly plane. If you feel comfortable with this, please use this technique. To start, however, I suggest applying the oil without a set method. Get into your thoughts and desires while applying the oil. Envision your request and the purpose of the candle being sent heavenward and then coming back to you in the form of your desired blessing. If you have decided that more than one oil is appropriate to your purpose, try to narrow it down to two. Put one on the candle and drip the other (the core of the issue) down the wick into the core of the candle.

It's important to concentrate and envision what you want to bring into your life upon each application. Think or say an informal prayer or description of what you would like. Make lists if it makes your request clearer to you. Envision your wish coming true for the highest good of *all* involved. Thank whomever you believe in spiritually.

If you choose to use glitter in the preparation of your magical candles, the oil is the magical ingredient that makes the glitter stick to the candle's surface.

LIGHT INCENSE

You can use incense in your candle preparation to set the tone of the request. The smoke covers the candle as you insert it into a jar or tall glass holder and bathes it in the atmosphere you desire. Is it an atmosphere of trust, new beginnings, or luck? If you are not using a jar, light incense in your room for the same purpose.

Place ¼ to ½ teaspoon of powdered incense into a spoon and light it. With the spoon, trace an invoking pentagram and three circles of completion (clockwise) around the top of the candle glass. You can use circles or any form you feel is appropriate. Angle the spoon into the glass so you can blow out the powdered incense safely. This will also prevent it from extinguishing when it hits the bottom of the jar. Once it is out and smoldering, empty the spoon's contents into the glass. Cover the top of the glass with your hand and let the smoke accumulate in the jar. When you feel the smoke is at the right density, angle the candle into the jar, being careful not to smear your glitter, if used.

GLITTER THE SEAL

Glitter is an optional but very nice enhancement. You can buy glitter from art supply and drug stores. The smaller the flakes, the easier the glitter is to handle. There are many different methods for applying the glitter to the surface of the candle. In order to follow the carved outlines of the seal, some people fold a sheet of paper, pour glitter into the fold, and tap it onto the surface of the candle. Some people put the glitter in small jars with a hole out of which a controlled stream of glitter can flow.

David Schulhoff

It is easier to outline the seals by tapping the glitter flakes directly onto the candle's surface, rather than working above it without touching the candle. Clean up stray glitter with your finger. Each time you tap out about one to two inches of glitter outline, while holding the candle, remove excess glitter by turning your wrist out 45 degrees away from you (like quickly flicking off a fly). The hardest thing to remember is to hold the candle in a way that your hand does not get in the glitter while you are working on it.

~ MAKE WISHES ~

Now you can make wishes that will come true every day—not just on your birthday. Make lists of the aspects of your wishes and read them each time you light your candle. Do whatever it takes to get clear and concentrated energy into the candle. If you are using a jar, a good way to make wishes with your candle is to drop an appropriate number of pennies (or any copper coin) into the jar. With each penny, make a wish.

Choose the number of coins that corresponds to your purpose:

0 Beyond the beginning
1 Individuality, autonomy, unification
2 Duality, union of two, knowledge
3 Unite two to form another entity
4 Structure, hard work, formation
5 Change, attraction and finding
6 Success, harmony
7 Soul development, spiritual enlightenment
8 Balance, judgment
9 Attain goals, completion
10 Completed force, back to the beginning—back to the one

If you do not have a jar, write down your wishes and concentrate on each one.

~ Think of what you like and envision your desire coming true.

~ Always add the spiritual disclaimer stating that the wish will be for the highest good of all involved.

~ Also add that if it manifests differently from how you request it, that you are strong and flexible enough to embrace the manifestation as the blessing you have been seeking. This could be a different kind of healing or an even better mate coming your way (even though you had your eye on a special someone), etc. Sometimes death is a form of healing. Something unexpected comes along and is the best thing. In other words, we don't always know what is the best thing for us. We can ask for what we think is the best thing, but be open to how the best thing arrives . . .

~ BURN THE CANDLE ~

You can burn it little by little. Each time you light the candle you are renewing the energy of your request through your attention. You do not have to focus on it all the time, but it is nice if it can be burning while you are in the house. When you leave, *always* extinguish all candles. When you put it out by blowing or smothering it (whichever you prefer), please thank whomever you believe in and whoever spiritually helps you with your request, even if you have not seen the results yet. See the "Hows, Whens, and What Ifs" section below, for questions covering issues such as how long to keep a candle lit and how to extinguish it.

~ LIGHT A CANDLE FOR THANKS ~

Even if you only see the first step, say "thank you" for what you received. If you cannot see that anything happened, reexamine the situation. Did *anything* happen? Most people can find something, but often discount it, particularly if there was a bad result, not enough of a good result, or an outcome they had not envisioned. Find the good in whatever happened. It is for the good, even if you cannot see the bigger picture yet. So much of what happens in our lives happens to strengthen us, bring clarity, and help us make the best choices. Some people are afraid that if they stop and give thanks, the blessings will stop. Just the opposite will happen.

After your candle finishes, it is good to pause and be grateful for the blessings given and what you have. The last symbol in this book, on page 201, is a symbol you can carve on a candle for thanks. The names of the gods and goddesses used in the illustration are merely suggestions. Fill in your religious pantheon (God, Jesus, the Holy Ghost or Virgin Mary, any god, goddess, or aspects of Buddha, Allah, Jehovah, or Krishna, etc.) or even your friends who helped you spiritually.

It is not necessary to use the symbol; you can carve into the wax the words describing for what you are grateful. This candle is not to ask for anything, but to give thanks after you burn a candle for a wish to come true.

~ HOWS, WHENS, AND WHAT IFS OF CANDLE BURNING ~

Does the way a candle burns have meaning?

We are told what is happening and will happen with our wishes, if we listen and watch the way the candle burns . . . and what it leaves behind.

As the candle burns, examine *how* it burns; it will tell you something about the task. A candle changes things, but also tells you what will happen and is happening in the way it burns. It can show how the request is going, being received, will turn out, and how hard it is to achieve.

Examine the candle glass and be open to the impressions and messages you get. How did your candle burn? Did it keep going out? Did it burn slowly or quickly? Did the flame flicker? Did it burn cleanly or give off soot? Again, meditate upon what message you get about how it burned. Did the glitter or wax stick to the glass? Meditate on the shapes and colors left there. Can you see any forms or symbols in the wax left on the glass? Try to figure out what the shapes suggest. If, for example, much of the wax stuck to the glass, maybe your request is not so straightforward or maybe it's a sticky situation.

As a general guideline, think positively first. That may be hard to do faced with any emotional issue.

What a candle does is not a "bad" sign:

If it gives off soot, you are burning off the negativity and obstacles surrounding your issue. Keep burning a candle about the issue until it burns cleanly.

If it flickers, your candle is working hard. Perhaps there is some vacillation in the progress or even in your own mind.

Did it burn slowly or go out? The task may require a slow and careful process. Or there could be numerous obstacles to overcome and the candle is laboring with all its might. It may also be indicating that you need to reassess the way you are thinking about your request. Maybe things have changed since you started the candle. Maybe you are not thinking of the highest good of all parties involved. Candles can, in those circumstances, go out. If this happens, it is part of your symbolic work to relight it and think about the issues at hand. Spiritual work takes participation. The candle may need your help to keep working and overcoming obstacles. You might need to dig wax out or dislodge the wick. This might require carving down the outer sides of the candle. Never pour off the center; it creates a bigger hole in which to drown your wick. Keep lighting it and working with it.

Sometimes, a candle keeps going out, reflecting a bigger process. There may be an issue of your fate and more at hand than your wish. Perhaps you do a candle to keep your job and it keeps going out. The candle could be indicating what is happening. The bosses are deciding to fire you. *A single candle sometimes cannot overcome massively dire circumstances that may be part of propelling you into evolving. Keep in mind that your candle may not give you all the steps of the specific wish, but it will take care of you. Keep your eyes open for the steps to your goal. Even if you cannot see the good in whatever happens, know it will come. Have faith.*

If it burned quickly, the task could have needed fast energy. It could have consumed the offered energy as rapidly as it was manufactured. On the other hand, it could have burned quickly because the goal was straightforward and easy.

Did it explode or did the glass break? To me, this usually means that my request is finalized and will happen. It could also reflect a highly explosive situation. It might also mean your request is misguided. Search within yourself for the truth.

Did it burn beautifully, but you did not get what you asked for? Usually candles do bring something. It may not be what you asked for, but something changed. Did you get the first step in your request or did you get something that was even better than you initially wanted? If you still feel nothing happened, examine your goal. Is it for the highest good of all involved? Is it the end of the road, not the beginning? In other words, do you want fame, even before you've done the work?

On the other hand, did you get what you wished for before the candle was finished? Continue the candle. There could be more blessings around you to come.

Did your wish change midway through? Did you break up? Did you not want the boyfriend, job, car, or apartment anymore? Even if you feel the opposite happened or your goal was misdirected, continue with the candle. Never reject the candle. It's a matter of respect. The candle helped to change your mind or move your life in a better direction. Have faith, continue the candle, and be open to the lessons and blessings to come.

How long should my candle be lit?

Many people believe that candles are more powerful if left burning. I understand that this may be certain peoples' traditions and belief systems. So, if you are comfortable with this, please do it with maximum safety. Never leave candles on or near surfaces such as wood, plastic, or fabric. Put the candle in a bowl of water, in a bathtub with no curtains around it, or in a sink with nothing that can fall on it. Even then, I advise against leaving it burning. Because of cats, children, and the nature of fire, I strongly believe that candles should be put out when you leave your room or house. Also, leaving a candle burning when you have some fear about it is undoing whatever good the candle could do. You may get your wish, but cause a huge loss by fire. It's not worth it. If there is an emergency situation, such as needing the rent in a few days or courage and luck during a court appearance or job interview, and you want to leave it burning, have a friend watch it when you cannot.

The tradition of leaving a candle burning originated before electricity. To me, in this age, leaving it burning is a fear-based superstition. The energy with your candle does not decrease when you put it out. The flame is a symbol, not the only force. In the same way, if the flame goes out, it tells you something about your request. It does not indicate it's over. Because they are in some way spooked, some people throw out their candle if it goes out. This is very disrespectful. Continue all candles to the end; they have more to give. This is discussed further on page 33, in the section called, "How soon will my candle work?"

Candle work is a process and usually more than seven days are required for the fulfillment of the task. Putting a candle out does not reduce its power. It may, actually, increase your participation and, thereby, increase its effectiveness. Your request may not be able to be done in the time it takes to burn the candle, and the concentration of energy may be too much for your request. Unless it is an unusual circumstance, I prefer to light and relight a candle. Remember, however, when you extinguish a candle, thank whoever spiritually helps you with your request, even if you have not seen the results yet. When you relight it, reaffirm what the candle is for.

What is the best way to extinguish a candle?

Some people prefer snuffing out, rather than blowing out, a candle, fearing that the blowing blows away the magic. In contrast, I believe that you are adding your breath to the magic.

Whatever deepens your connection to the candle enhances the intent. The bottom line is, use whichever method you feel is respectful to your purpose and the candle.

How soon will my candle work?

It varies. Candles may work before you light them, during the burning, when it ends, or a time later. I had one candle achieve its goal while it was still in my handbag, heading home. Often, you are so clear in your intention, your goal manifests posthaste. Results can also occur gradually during the burning of the candle or when the candle completely burns out. It can come after one week, one month, or longer. It depends upon the magnitude and grantability of your request. That is why I suggest that you conquer the steps along the way to achieving your goal, instead of heading for marriage, fame, big cash, or whatever your ultimate goal is. Don't always run to do another candle. Wait. Have faith. The magic doesn't end when the flame does. (That is why you can put a candle out and have it still be as strong.) On the other hand, if the request is big, ongoing, or has great obstacles, be persistent and do another candle based on what you have learned with the first one.

Always finish all candles. As mentioned above, it is a matter of respect. Even if you have already achieved your goal or feel that the purpose was misdirected, burn the candle to the end. If your goals have changed, alter or add to your wishes accordingly. Maybe your goal is not complete or maybe the process of burning the candle changed you and the goal. Maybe there is more to learn. Also, you never know what additional blessings could be in store for you!

What if I can't draw?

The request will not backfire if you could not make it look like the picture of the seal in this book. *It does not matter if you can draw well* or if the note you write in the wax is legible. It is important to focus on the task and try your best. When drawing the seals, your intention and focus have therapeutic and spiritual impact. If you feel really blocked and negative or cannot carve because of a physical disability, have someone who believes in the best for you carve the candle.

Can I do this wrong and ruin things?

You're still sure that you did something wrong . . .

If you do a step differently or with different ingredients, it is not wrong. Many people feel a spell didn't work because they made a mistake in the steps. The only mistakes would be a lack of ethics, lack of clarity in intent, or lack of openness to see what the universe *did* bring. Examine whether your request takes into account what is for the highest good of all involved. Candles are used to remove worry, not make you obsessed with the purpose. Try to see what the candle is telling you—and think positively! If you do not get what you want, examine why it may not be the best thing for you.

What if I did not get what I wanted?

It may seem that your candle did not work. I encourage you to be very open to the ways the answer to your candle manifests. It is not always the way we envision it. In addition, it may be only the first step. Be glad the steps are being made. Your request may not be able to be answered in a brief time. Part of this process is acknowledging and enjoying the process.

When should I light the candle?

You can light a candle anytime you need to a wish to come true.

The most important aspect of Candle Therapy is having the "quality time" to spend with our candle. In addition, there does not have to be a flame for your candle to be working. Some people insist that they must leave a candle burning during a job interview or an important meeting with a lover. I don't recommend ever leaving an unattended candle burning, but if you feel you must, leave it with a friend to watch over.

If you would like to fine-tune your candle burning, you can light your candle on the right day of the week for your purpose. Historically, the names of the days were derived from the planet that ruled it. For example, Sunday is the day of the sun. The origins of some of the days of the week stemmed from the names of the gods or goddesses that were associated with particular planets.

Days	Planet	Colors	Named for	Purpose
Monday	Moon	(silver/white)	Moon day	Peace, protection, emotional healing
Tuesday	Mars	(red)	Tiw's day	Motivation, strength, power, sex
Wednesday	Mercury	(orange/yellow/gray)	Woden's day	Communication, success, writing
Thursday	Jupiter	(purple/blue)	Thor's day	Expansion, enlightenment, justice
Friday	Venus	(pink/green)	Freya or Frigg's day	Attraction of love or money
Saturday	Saturn	(black/brown)	Saturn or Seterne's day	Finalizations, reductions, wisdom
Sunday	Sun	(yellow/orange)	Sun day	Blessings, success, joy, love, money

Once you get a feeling for the meaning of the planets, you will decide what day in which to light your candle. In general, healings are favorable on Mondays or Fridays; love on Fridays or Sundays; protection on Mondays or Tuesdays; court cases on Tuesdays or Thursdays; opportunities, communication, getting a point across, blessing the skills of a surgeon, or finding a new job or apartment on Wednesdays; business deals can be best done on Tuesday, Wednesday or Thursday; and lust on Tuesday, Friday, or Sunday.

You can also light it during an appropriate phase of the moon.

THE MOON

The moon is an age-old symbol that has represented everything from protection to danger. The phases are essential cycles to which human events and earthly rhythms are bound. For example, a woman's menstrual cycle can follow the moon cycle. A woman often ovulates or menstruates on the new or full moons. From moon to moon was a "period." That's why a woman's bleeding time is called a period. The word "month" came from the Latin word *mensis*. Its plural is menses. "Mens" in Latin refers to moon, mind, and spiritual power. The Roman goddess Mensa, like moon goddess Minerva, measured time. In addition, the old calendar was thirteen months, following the number of moon and menstrual cycles. Therefore, the number thirteen got a bad reputation as the world shifted from a matriarchal to patriarchal society.

The moon was the romantic symbol, in the movies, by which Astaire and Rogers danced and Cary Grant charmed. The moon turned actors into werewolves; the metal that was sacred to the moon—silver—killed them.

Not only actors and werewolves were affected; the moon influences us all. The tides, as well as the fluids within people, are pulled by the moon's influence.

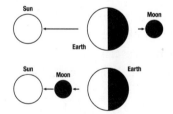

Tides are highest when the sun and moon work together and line up.

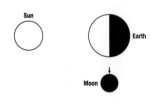

Tides are weakest when their pulls work against each other.

Biologically, the movement and balance of fluid is one of the most important aspects of maintaining homeostasis, a state of equilibrium. Therefore, it would make sense that the moon cycle influences health, both emotional and physical. In ancient times, when people were affected too much, they were called lunatics. During full moons (the time when the moon's gravitation pull is the greatest), crimes and births increase. Emergency rooms get busier.

In the old religions (pagan, goddess-oriented, etc.), the moon has always been mother, protector, and a fertility symbol. Multitudinous cultures have gathered their omens from the moon and her movements. Farmers plant by the moon. Sailors navigate by her. She lights paths and protects travelers because she brings the hidden to light.

PHASES OF THE MOON AND CANDLES

The moon follows a 29.5-day cycle. There are approximately fourteen to fifteen days from new moon to full moon. As a brief rule of thumb, it is good to carve candles to build a situation on a new or full moon and to send something away from you on a waning moon.

~ *The new moon* is the time to emphasize and inspire *new beginnings* and lasts for fourteen to fifteen days until the full moon. It is a time to build and activate. The new moon is the start of the *waxing* moon (when it is building and getting bigger). If you do a candle for drawing money from the new moon to full moon, meditate on your money increasing. To anthropomorphize the moon, think of the new moon as a young maiden growing into the full, ripe maid. Since whatever you do on the new moon sets the tone for the time up until the full, try to make the day of the new moon a good one. If, for example, you fight with your mate on the new moon, most likely you will be working things out for the next fourteen and a half days until the full moon.

Waxing Moon

Waning Moon

~ *The full moon* is the peak of the moon's building power. Often the things begun on the new moon culminate at this time. This moon is as fertile as the maid at ovulation.

~ *The waning moon* occurs after the moon is full and she starts to wane or reduce in size. Waning occurs from the time of the full to the dark moon (when the moon becomes the crone). It is a good time to let go and release. Get rid of obstacles, negativity, hurt, relationships, or unwanted pounds. You can also do a money candle, for example, when waning. Just focus on waning away poverty and fears surrounding money. Therefore, any candle can be done at anytime; *it's your meditation that must change.*

~ *The dark moon* is a very magical time right before the new moon, when the moon is invisible in the sky. It appears that the moon has waned away. It is the time of dark goddesses, crone energy, and female mysteries. The Crone is the wise woman, the knower of all mysteries—the invisible. Also, since the moon is such a powerful feminine force, it is a good time to acknowledge the mystery and power of womanhood.

THE INFLUENCE OF THE PLANETS ON THE MOON

The moon travels through the twelve zodiacal signs in its monthly cycle. Astrological calendars will help you follow this movement. Noting which planet the moon is in at any given time is enhancing, but not totally necessary, to Candle Therapy. If you are doing some magic that pertains directly to the moon and her power, you might want to light the candle during a planetary influence that suits your purpose.

The following is a list of the moon's attributes and what aspects of life it influences as it travels through the following signs:

THE MOON'S ATTRIBUTES AND INFLUENCES	
Aries	Promoting energy and ideas. Initiating projects.
Taurus	Money, stability, and sensuality.
Gemini	Communication, wit, magnetism, verbal and written expression, business dealings, entertainment, and charm.
Cancer	Domestic affairs, blessings to the home, and watery emotions.
Leo	Success in the arts and entertainment, dynamism, healing, the energy of the sun, recognition, and courage.
Virgo	Verbal and written expression (stimulating and overcoming writer's block), healing, school, concerns of the home and hearth, mental and detail-oriented work, and understanding.
Libra	Balance, stability, harmony, justice, and innovation.
Scorpio	Transformation, change, lust, intensity, secrets, self-exploration, and strong decision making.
Sagittarius	Travel, socialness, increased energy, outdoors, and warm initiation of action.
Capricorn	Business, things of the earth, money, grounding, and success.
Aquarius	Higher mind, intellectualism, and trance work.
Pisces	Spirituality, dreams, psychic work, sensitivity, contemplation, fantasy, imagination, rest, insight, and intuition.

What should I do with the candle once it's done?

It is good to let go of the candle when it is done. It is an expression of faith. When it finishes, kiss the glass and thank whatever higher force helped you achieve your goal. Place some offering (coins, petals, or another token of your appreciation) in the bottom of the glass or on what's left of the glass. Place it in a separate bag from your garbage and place it in a recycling bin. Although it is spiritually correct to return a magical request to living water or the earth, waxes and magical remnants are now pollution. Most candles are petroleum products. (If you think about it, our dumping is in the ocean or landfills, so your candle does end up returning to the earth or water anyway. But it is better to recycle it.) Please choose the most ecologically kind way to dispose of your candles!

Another approach for marking the end of your candle is used by one of my colleagues. He breaks the glass, signifying a letting go and end of the magical working. For those of us who are accident prone and concerned about the trash handlers, please proceed with care. Please cover your eyes and hands. Also, please package the remains so you don't hurt a sanitation worker.

~ WHAT TO DO IF IT SEEMS YOUR CANDLE DID NOT WORK ~

1. *Review Hows, Whens, and What Ifs on page 30.*
2. *Reassess the way you are thinking about your request.* Maybe you are not clear or your intent isn't pure. Assess your agenda and what is best for all. Stay open to other things happening. It may not be exactly the way you envision it.
3. *Always burn a candle to the end.* Your goal may change midway through. You may be tempted to think that the candle did not work if a candle brings you different results from what was first intended. Say you had your eye on a man whom you wanted as a boyfriend. If it was revealed during the process of burning your candle that the guy you wanted was a jerk, you might be tempted to throw out the candle. But think—it may have eliminated months of hell and time wasted. By the time it has burned away, you may have your eye on someone better. The candle definitely worked by showing you the first person wasn't your mate and, then, bringing the best love to you.
4. *Respect and love your candle.* Your candle is a tool that is trying to help you. In my experience, some people become frustrated with their candles. It is easy to project your feelings about a situation onto the candle. See if you can discover the steps to deal with the source of frustration in the external world. Know that your candle is your helper. Try not to reject what helps.
5. *Discover what has happened toward your goal.* Initially, it may seem that nothing is happening to further your goals. Was what happened different from what you expected? Did a thing you didn't want to happen occur? The best result for us is not always the path we envision. Know that this result could be the first step to the rest of your *true* goal.

6. *Find something for which to be grateful.* For some of us being grateful is a daily routine. We glance around and give thanks for even the smallest things. You may not feel the blessings from your candle are what you wanted or good enough, so gratefulness and thanks are not in order. Some people say that they have nothing in their lives for which to be grateful. They may prove this with a large list of negatives. When you point out that they are healthy, have a house, or something else seemingly smaller, they can outline what falls short about those things too. But thanking whomever helps us spiritually for each step helps us in so many ways. We have to open our eyes to see our blessing. The smallest blessings can be the greatest ones.

7. *Do the candle work yourself.* The strength of Candle Therapy is doing your own carving and focusing, if possible. Physical disabilities may prevent doing all the rituals described in this book. In addition, you may have emotional issues that block your optimism of faith in yourself. I encourage you to gain clarity through speaking to a psychologist or a close friend. If you are still unclear, consider many different approaches to your issue. Read the choices in this book and do your preparation for the ritual. The procedures may resolve the fears. If you cannot figure out how to proceed, you can visit my stores or contact us by mail or e-mail; see page 223. You will find experienced people there who will be objective and really care about doing the best candle and magical work for you.

8. *Follow your intuition.* As long as a ritual is done with respect, you probably made no errors. Follow your intuition. In the 1970s, when I first learned to meditate, I naively asked a friend of mine whom I consider a true master, "When you are meditating and a fly lands on your nose, what do you do?" He smiled wisely and answered simply, "Flick it off." Because a step is not in the spiritual manual, it does not mean that your intuition and common sense take a hike. Some of magic and psychology, for that matter, is "winging it" and sensing what is the best move or judgment.

We are human, therefore, we want what we want, but . . .
Leave yourself open to other possibilities and what the universe will bring.

PART III

◆

LOVE

In this section, I will address the beginning of love, what you do once you have your lover, what to do if you lose your lover, and what to do if love doesn't arrive! A list of love oils and their meanings are at the end of this chapter.

Have you ever been in love? Really in love? Do you feel that love now? Is that person cherishing you and considering you as a priority? What do you love about him or her? Why do you respect them? What are your needs and are they being met? Do they call you enough? Is the communication good? Is the person available? If not, do you have a convincing justification for why that is okay? Can you answer these questions? How many are yeses?

Of course, every relationship, no matter how fine, has a couple of problems. The issues revolve around how hard you have to work to make the relationship work. It doesn't have to be vastly difficult. To be loved, you don't have to get yelled at. Love means never having to be struck or beaten. You don't have to carry the entire weight of the relationship. If you are with someone who is like that, they don't have to change—your relationship does, however. Either you both need to communicate your needs and create mutual consideration or you may have to let go. Sometimes change or leveling the faulty foundation is necessary so a better foundation can be built.

Love is:
~ not wondering if he or she will call, loves you, etc.
~ not feeling bad, unless it's a temporary thing about which you have to talk. Things do come up.
~ an experience that brings out the best in you.

41

~ being able to communicate openly and with constructive honesty. We often want people to be honest with us, but are we being honest with them? Even if you can justify why you are bending the truth to your lover, you are not being honest. The way you are sets the tone. They will never be honest as long as you are not. If being honest will make your relationship end, maybe he or she is not the one for you.

~ understanding they are a different person with different styles of expression. These styles may not be the same as yours.

~ understanding they are not going to change. Can you accept them as they are?

~ wanting to be faithful without pressure or rules.

~ paying attention to each other and being partners. The definition of being a team will be different for each person. Be sure to talk about it.

~ LOVE IS A MUTUAL DECISION ~

The key to keeping a relationship fresh and alive on a long-term basis is being aware of the above points (and many others). *In addition, both parties have to want to be in love.* Then, being in love can last forever. Build a relationship on joy and shared experiences and both of you will want to be in love.

Love magic is particularly difficult to do, because often there is an element of manipulation inherent in the act or way of thinking. In Candle Therapy, the recipes for love-related issues have no manipulative intent. Manipulation occurs during your assessment of goals, meditation, and the way you envision the relationship. Remember, for love to be true, your lover must come to you willingly. Love comes from shared experiences and joy. For your own self-esteem and trust in that person, it is important that they freely want to be with you. Never bind a person to you, manipulate his or her feelings, or break up another person's relationship. It is your job to assess what you want and how to get it ethically. For example, if your boyfriend is with another woman, do not separate them. Work on your attractiveness and self-esteem. Also, heal whatever is keeping you apart. Perhaps, he will come back. Before performing the following magical tasks, please read the Ethics section on page 9 and *be careful: Going against someone else's will (asserting your agenda and timing on a developing relationship) is a manipulative way to use candles and will backfire! If you force something, the person may run. Candles enhance what should be.*

Do not manipulate or force another to be in love with you—even if you determine it is fate for you to be together. Let what is supposed to happen—happen. Not your will. It's a relationship of two. If you are saying that they don't know what they want or are unable to do what you want them to, examine why you want to be with them and how any pressure may be counterproductive to your goal. Having someone against their will (by enchanting them with a "magic spell," as in the movies) is like not having them at all. The magic must be renewed constantly and you will never be sure if it is your magic or true love operating. Ultimately, it would not be rewarding to know (in your heart) that your lover is there because you are magically persuading him or her to be. In addition, *whatever you do magically comes back to you three times.*

You may sense that you have met the perfect mate. Yet, they are not responding the way you would like. Be patient. Love is a process and does not always proceed at your pace.

But, say you feel close before they do:

Maybe you feel close because of intimate experience. Intimacy and sexuality may feel like true knowledge, but it is not complete knowledge. The knowledge can reveal the person on a spiritual level. Yet, if we become intimate too fast, it may be difficult to reverse the process and fill in the smaller, everyday experiences that bring full knowledge of the other person.

You may believe in past lives and "soul mates" through time. You are in this life now. You are experiencing this set of experiences. Even if you feel there are past-life explanations (karmic debt), do not assume the other person is operating under the same assumptions. Remember, the *spirit of love* can take many forms. According to theories about past lives, soul mates are not always lovers. Deep familiarity can stem from meeting some close past connection, such as a fond sibling or parent. We can romanticize instant closeness for many current reasons; try to be objective as possible. If you are lonely or missing a connection with a parent, lover, or friend, try not to relegate the soul mate to fill that spot. Sometimes we identify the one aspect of a person, the way we feel around them, or other signs that say this is "the one." That is a good start, but don't bank on just that—now form a wealth of experiences in the real world. Don't close your eyes to what about the person does not fit into the profile of someone who loves you. Make decisions based on *all* the information. You deserve to be loved now and in this life—that is fate. We just have to choose wisely and keep trying. It is important to come to terms with how this connection is being built in the here-and-now, not the past.

One of the greatest problems in love magic is *patience* and *respecting that other people love, feel things, and trust at different paces.* Each of us has very necessary defensive structures that make us trust and care at different times. Don't force the progress of a relationship. It will be real and true if it progresses at its natural pace.

Okay, right, you understand, but you want this person! *Now, what can you do magically?*

- ~ Enhance what attraction and communication is there.
- ~ Clarify what each of you feels and why you are apart (if you are).
- ~ Heal the existing problems and reduce misunderstanding.
- ~ Foster trust and a willingness to communicate by letting go of your agenda.
- ~ Be honest.
- ~ Have fun and do things together.

~ THE PROCESS OF LOVE ~

The process of finding a new love is an external and internal quest. Although it may not seem like it, external factors are the easiest and least cumbersome obstacles to overcome. If one is internally (emotionally and spiritually) ready, the externals will fall into place. This symbol can help synthesize these processes with people you know or have yet to meet.

Whether you want a new love or have someone in mind, we want good love in our lives. The essence of this candle is to bring the right love to you. Ask for the good love you deserve! Reexamine and be open to changing some of your rules about meeting another person. Maybe the sparks won't fly the second you see each other. Maybe you have a "type" and you won't recognize that this person possesses the qualities you have requested. Keep your eyes open; they may be different from what you expect.

Listen to exactly what the person says. They will tell you about themselves. Don't see potentials or what they meant to say. If the person says, "I can't keep or don't want a relationship," believe them. If they are dishonest, abusive, disrespectful to you or them, or make you feel bad in any way—run. Remember, you are a treasure and anyone who doesn't know that doesn't deserve your love. If you feel any doubt about being a treasure, carve a candle for "Confidence and Self-Esteem," "Elimination of Fear," or "Emotional Healing."

Whatever we do in a relationship builds it. We cannot go back to the beginning because in the meantime, we have constructed something together. Ideally, we can choose to heal the relationship with mutual levels of responsibility and honesty. Do both of you have reasons not to trust the other? Have either of you cheated, lied, been too dependent, or had ulterior motives for the relationship (such as financial security)? Do either of you distrust that the other will give and respect space? Do you both have independent activities and respect the other's right to be separate? If either of you is away, does the other person panic and distrust? Can you figure out a way that both of you could build security for the other person? You, with or without your loved one, might seek therapy so you can feel safer and more trusting. If you truly feel the other person won't trust, commit, or whatever you feel would meet your need (and you have expressed your need clearly), you might have to face moving on from the relationship. If you cannot solve your problems so that your relationship is mutually enhancing and fun, then you might have to try symbols such as "Letting Go of Old or Present Love" or "Love Uncrossing and Clearing."

∼ FINDING AND ATTRACTING
THE BEST LOVE (NEW OR NOT) ∼

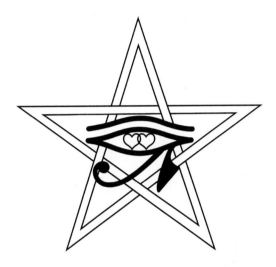

If you want to meet a new love and don't have anyone in mind, first envision who would be a good match for you. Write a description of the love you want (e.g., "soul mate," "life partner," "best love for now,") and list the qualities of the ideal person on paper. This is a good way to enhance your focus. You can also read and add to the list as your candle burns. Be thorough but not rigid. If they are important to you, don't forget things such as good sense of humor, mutual attraction and love, good health, faithful (remember, these things must be mutual; you are making a commitment, too), employed (or at least has enough money for their own dinner), available, and whatever else suits you. Read this list when you relight the candle. You can also carve this list, clockwise, into the wax, along the outlines of the star. For identification, include your name and astrological sign on the candle.

If you already know the person you want, put your name on the candle and then write his or her name and astrological sign. Under his or her name, write "or someone even better. For the highest good of us both. Thank you." Alternatively, you can write, "Please bring me my best love, if it is _____, please heal the situation (if applicable) and remove the obstacles to our love. If it is not, please bring me whoever is best as soon as possible. Thank you." Even though, right now, you really want this person, you never know what fate has in store for you.

IDEAL TIMING:
New Moon, Sunday, or Friday.

SUGGESTED CANDLE AND GLITTER COLORS:

Yellow is for joy and is the best choice for bringing the best love to you on a soul mate level. Out of joy comes friendship. Out of friendship comes true lasting romance! Pink or green are the colors of Venus, for long-lasting love. Pink is more romantic, but that's not all you want; be sure to specify in your meditation that you want the joy and friendship, too. Green is for a firm foundation and growth. You can use red for lust and passion. It's good for getting someone's attention in a pushy way. But be careful; it can be too pushy and feel like pressure. Wait for a good foundation before using red.

OILS AND/OR INCENSES:

Venus, Joy and Contentment, Bliss, Faith, Bast, Love Potion 131, Courting, Attract Soul Mate Romance, or Long-Lasting Love

MEDITATION:

After soaking in the tub or quieting yourself in some way, write on a piece of paper the qualities you would like your new love to have. If you already know the person, still write a list, even if the person you like doesn't have those qualities. There is a great deal to learn from writing down what you want. Also include what you would like to happen. Read over the paper. Try to be bluntly honest with yourself. Is this the best person for you? Why? Are they showing it? After you examine that, feel yourself being washed with warm love. Envision the perfect love coming to you as if from above, into your life. If you are heading toward marriage, see the love growing before *and after* the marriage. Please say "please" and "thank you" to whomever you believe in and whoever spiritually helps you with your request. Always emphasize that you understand that this is merely a request—a strong request—but you know that whatever happens is for the highest good and may not manifest exactly as you envision it.

ADDITIONAL SUGGESTIONS:

Take a soothing bath with chamomile and lavender thrown into it. Envision your true love. Feel the security of true love around you as the warm water bathes you.

~ MAKING YOURSELF MORE ATTRACTIVE AND IRRESISTIBLE ~

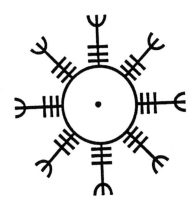

The perfume industry is based upon attraction and making you more glamorous. The manufacturers don't worry about the magical implications, but you should. If you have someone in mind, using this seal can be considered manipulative, unless you add a spiritual disclaimer of sorts. If you find yourself focusing upon attracting a specific person, add a thought to your meditation that this is what *you* want. Wanting to attract him or her is not wrong; just add that you will accept whatever happens, for the highest good of all involved (them *and* you). You cannot know what is their fate or what is the best for them. Leave it to the higher forces. Carve your name, astrological sign, and this symbol on any candle. If you have someone in mind, use that name, but add the phrase "or someone *even* better." Be sure to write "please" as you start and "thank you" at the end. For irresistibility that will knock 'em dead, even without a specific person in mind, use this ancient Icelandic symbol. It can help to make you confident and alluring.

IDEAL TIMING:

New moon.

SUGGESTED CANDLE AND GLITTER COLORS:

Pink for sending out sweet affection and approachable signals. Red for being a fireball and white for purity and light. You can also try your favorite or a color that speaks to you.

OILS AND/OR INCENSES:

Choose one of these to make you irresistible! Irresistibility, Glamour and Seduction, Come to Me, Cardamon, Cleopatra, Mysterious, Venus, Voodoo Nights Sex, Khus Khus, Attraction, Ylang Ylang or VaVoom.

MEDITATION:

When you light the candle or soak in the tub, meditate upon how good you feel being attractive. Do this for yourself and people will notice. Feel yourself becoming more glamorous and interesting. See yourself being more confident and beautiful around people. Please say "please" and "thank you" to whomever you believe in and whoever spiritually helps you with your request. Always emphasize that you understand that this is merely a request—a strong request—but you know that whatever happens is for the highest good and may not manifest exactly as you envision it.

ADDITIONAL SUGGESTIONS:

Prepare yourself for attracting love by taking a bath in lovage herb or splashing on a love oil of your choosing. Sprinkle rose petals around the room to which you want to attract someone. You can sprinkle Irresistibility or Kindly Spirit powders in a room to charm a crowd.

You can also photocopy or hand-copy this seal and carry it until your dream comes true. When you feel your attractiveness and you get the proof, burn it and send up your thanks for this gift.

~ WHAT TO DO ONCE YOU HAVE A LOVE ~

Now you have a love! The following are suggestions and seals that may be appropriate, depending upon the depth and duration of your relationship.

You may sense that you have met the perfect mate. Yet, they are not responding the way you would like. People know and feel things at different times. Be sure to respect that each person has necessary defensive structures; people trust and care at different paces. If the pace is interfered with, trust may not be solid. There is a rhythm.

It is sometimes hard to find the balance between respect and change in a relationship. We can be too retiring or too aggressive while participating in the relationship's growth. Respecting a person's process can turn into waiting too long for change, or wanting our vision of the changes to happen, we force things. Either way, things will not work out.

Relax and know if it is meant to be, both of you will grow in the ways you need in order to be together.

❧ DIFFERENT PROBLEMS AND HOW TO ADDRESS THEM WITH CANDLE THERAPY ❧

I have had many years of gathering peoples' experiences. Many things I describe may pertain to you or not; take from it what you will. My comments sound blunt, but they are based on happy success stories.

Sometimes, people try to recover the way love was in the beginning with that special someone. A relationship builds; beginning, middle, and present. The middle is something you can't (and I hope do not want to) erase. All the sections are important building blocks of whatever your relationship is. If you do not like the middle and present, heal them so your future is bright.

Maybe there is something about that person that is proof that they are your soul mate. Sometimes, we can believe that only that person can make us feel that way or have a certain quality. People hold on to that proof. In the meantime, the relationship can be faltering, if not downright horrible.

Many people who want to keep someone do so at the cost of expressing their own needs. Difficulties with the love may be trying to show you that you should make a very hard choice—in your best interest. At that point, use seals such as "Eliminate Fear and Insecurity," "Get Clarity About a Relationship," "Confidence and Self-Esteem," or "Strength." Is the universe, God, your inner self (or whomever you believe in) trying to show you that this is not your highest love? If you resolve to let go, there are seals to help do that, too, such as "Letting Go of Old or Present Love."

Be careful not to force your agenda. If you want them to commit before things are healed between you or their trust is in place, your impatience will backfire. Expressing our needs in a reasonable way can make us more of an individual to respect and love. Instead of asserting what must happen, try healing the situation and both of you with the "Love Healing" symbol on a green candle. Then see what happens. Change must occur on *both* sides for any true love to exist.

Then, ask yourself: Are you subjugating yourself to them in exchange for something? Do you have to give up too much in order to meet your needs for love or money? You can do this differently. It takes bravery, but it will result in a better path for you.

Sometimes, people do not want to take the steps it requires to have a relationship. One has to talk and heal the problems first before walking down the aisle together. You may think that your loved one is not listening to you, but have you listened to them? Did your lover say, "I want space" or something else that you did not believe? Respect their boundaries and wishes and see if that gets you further than resisting their requests. It is possible that the space is the healing they need. They may need to figure out what they feel. They could relax and trust because you respected what they asked. In contrast, holding on to what you believe is what they meant or what is best for them in your eyes will choke the relationship's breath.

Honesty, trust, and respect have to happen from the beginning *and* throughout the relationship. If your relationship is fairly established, but you both never included the other in these steps, you can learn. On the other hand, it may be too late. But you can try by talking, going to therapy together, and using symbols such as "Increase Communication," "Increase Trust and Understanding," or "Get a Person to Sit Down and Talk About Difficulties." Remember: Everything is a two-way street.

Know when to heal and when to leave. Ask for the good love you deserve!

∼ ELIMINATE FEAR AND INSECURITY ∼

One of the most important factors in a successful relationship is getting rid of insecurity and fear. This seal is good for fears in relationships. For eliminating your personal fears and bringing happiness and joy, see "Elimination of Fear" on page 117.

This seal is for soothing fears in *both* parties. Remember, everything you do affects you, too. This is not the seal to carve if the other person is fearful about something you want (commitment, seeing you, etc.) Examine why the person has to have that boundary. See if you can approach the problem without your agenda and see how you can be healed and relax, too; perhaps that will help them trust you more. Carve your name, astrological sign, and wish in the wax. Be sure to write "please" as you start and "thank you" at the end.

IDEAL TIMING:
Anytime.

SUGGESTED CANDLE AND GLITTER COLORS:
Yellow or gold (sun). Red (Mars) if fear, self-love, and confidence are the main issues. Pink (Venus) for loving yourself and feeling confident.

OILS AND/OR INCENSES:
Joy and Contentment, Mars and Motivation, Camellia (or for women, Camellia mixed with Venus oil), Fearlessness and Confidence, or Love Openness (for you both).

MEDITATION:
Meditate upon building self-confidence, security, and self-love. If the moon is waxing, light the candle, feeling fearless and confident. If waning, send away feelings of self-doubt, fear

of judgment, and nervousness. Also, send obstacles and general fears away. Please say "please" and "thank you" to whomever you believe in and whoever spiritually helps you with your request. Always emphasize that you understand that this is merely a request—a strong request—but you know that whatever happens is for the highest good and may not manifest exactly as you envision.

ADDITIONAL SUGGESTIONS:

Take a bath in Fearlessness and Confidence oil. Throw petals from a red flower of your choosing into your tub for strength. Breathe in the strength as you relax in the tub. Release the fear with the release of the bathwater.

Photocopy or hand-copy this seal on parchment or rag bond. Carry it in a little bag with cloves, rosemary, frankincense, and one petal of the reddest rose you can find (for strength, fearlessness, and confidence). You can also add powdered nutmeg for communication and a dash of Fearlessness and Confidence incense. When you feel free of the fears in your relationship, burn the seal and send up your thanks for this gift. You can bury the bag by a tree in a beautiful place, as long as all the contents are biodegradable. Otherwise, fill it full of jewelry that holds meaning for you and treasure it.

∾ DEEPEN AND CONTINUE A RELATIONSHIP ∾

Of course, if nothing is wrong, there is no need to do any kind of fix-it candle. Are you just grateful for such a fine relationship? If so, do a thank-you candle (see page 201)!

On the other hand, your insecurities may be rising. You may feel the person needs to be closer to you. Perhaps you want a deeper commitment. That may very well be an appropriate step, but examine your motivations. Do you need a commitment so you won't lose the person? Is this too soon for a deeper step? Is it impatience on your part? Do you know each other well enough? A good relationship takes spending joyous time together, during which the person learns to trust, respect, and treasure you, by what you do. Building a good relationship is a process of building real trust and establishing ways of dealing with problems. You may need to use other symbols first such as "Increase Communication," "Stop Fighting and Stress," or "Increase Trust and Understanding."

Know that commitment does not immediately mean flowers and a ring. Issues that have been stopping the deepening will arise and sometimes not be pleasant. A fight might arise to clear the air of unsaid things before the commitment can occur. So, if you are dedicated to deepening, get ready to be open, honest, understanding, accepting, and not defensive. If you use this prematurely, it could feel like pressure to your loved one and, thus, backfire. Of course, you should mention to the other that it is your intention to be married (so they know). Then, let go of your pressure, enjoy the relationship, and get to know this person even better than you do. Unless you *both want to be married*, it won't work. People have different progressions. Be patient. Commitment is full of joy. You cannot force joy. Carve your name and astrological sign on the right of the candle under the circle and your love's name on the left side.

IDEAL TIMING:

Anytime.

SUGGESTED CANDLE AND GLITTER COLORS:

Gold or yellow for the sun. Silver or white for purity and openness. Green or pink for Venus. Green is the most natural choice for this candle, because it taps into the deeper aspects of the love goddess, Venus.

OILS AND/OR INCENSES:

Goona Goona, Joy and Contentment, Bliss, Blessed Light and Thanks, or Long-Lasting Love.

MEDITATION:

See yourself becoming more of a couple with the other person. Feel deepening trust and abiding love. Envision light and love around you both. Use the new to full moons to build and the waning moon to eliminate obstacles. Please say "please" and "thank you" to whomever you believe in and whoever spiritually helps you with your request. Always emphasize that you understand that this is merely a request—a strong request—but you know that whatever happens is for the highest good and may not manifest exactly as you envision it.

ADDITIONAL SUGGESTIONS:

Plant a plant for your relationship to continue to grow. Nurture it. You can also photo-copy or hand-copy this seal on parchment or rag bond. Carry it in a little bag with rosebuds and an orris root. You can also buy your candle flowers as an offering. When you aren't car-rying the bag, put it in a special place. When your love has moved to the next phase, burn the seal and send up your thanks for this gift. If you want, you can give the bag to your love. Explain that when they carry the bag, your love is with them.

∿ SPRUCE UP A RELATIONSHIP ∿

Are you missing the romance, attentiveness, and spontaneity of your lover? This is super for reawakening sensual excitement and pleasure. For even more titillation, tell your lover what you are doing and have your love carve his or her own name on the candle. Plan a special date. Please don't plan it without your lover knowing. This is not the time for surprises. It is time for openness and togetherness. Even dressing up and changing the setting for an evening will make your relationship more special. Put your names and astrological signs on the candle and relax into the vision of your happiness together.

IDEAL TIMING:
New and waxing moon.

SUGGESTED CANDLE AND GLITTER COLORS:
Gold or yellow for the renewal of the sun. Pink or green for the beauty and rich love of Venus. Red is for lust.

OILS AND/OR INCENSES:
Cleopatra, VaVoom, Glamour and Seduction, Courting, Aphrodisiac Potion, Sun, Voodoo Nights Sex, Verbena, Glitz, Fun and Lust, or Irresistibility.

MEDITATION:
Meditate upon sending away past and present obstacles (physical and mental) to the romance you envision for your present relationship. Feel the problems and blocks flowing easily off of you. Let them go. Envision light and love around you. Please say "please" and

"thank you" to whomever you believe in and whoever spiritually helps you with your request. Always emphasize that you understand that this is merely a request—a strong request—but you know that whatever happens is for the highest good and may not manifest exactly as you envision it.

ADDITIONAL SUGGESTIONS:

Prepare yourself for a fabulous time with your lover by taking a bath in a love oil of your choosing or red rose petals.

Put pink and yellow candles around the house to set an atmosphere of joy, love, and romance. Burn an incense such as Goona Goona (for trust and understanding) or Venus (for warmth and love). Concentrate on the best thing happening for both of you.

~ STABILIZE AN ERRATIC RELATIONSHIP ~

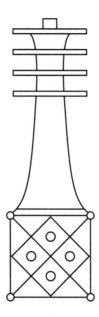

This is good for stabilizing the relationship and bringing more consistency. In a situation where the person appears and disappears, wish for more stability and communication. As always, carve your and your lover's names on the candle.

IDEAL TIMING:

Anytime.

SUGGESTED CANDLE AND GLITTER COLORS:

Avoid hot and fiery colors like red or yellow if there is anger. Use blue for peace. Pink for Venus and orange or copper for Mercury. White for purity and balance. Brown for grounding and stability. Green for healing and balance.

OILS AND/OR INCENSES:

If the problems are trust, understanding, and communication, use Goona Goona. If the difficulties revolve around enjoying each other, use Joy and Contentment oil. If you are opposite types of people, use Bay oil. If anger is an issue, use Anger Be Gone. Spikenard helps build the stability of a relationship.

MEDITATION:

If new or full moons, build, stabilize, increase communication, and enhance what is strong and healthy between you. If waning, send away problems and whatever hurts. Avoid wishing away other people in your lover's life. Stick to what is between you two and only about you two. Please say "please" and "thank you" to whomever you believe in and whoever spiritually helps you with your request. Always emphasize that you understand that this is merely a request—a strong request—but you know that whatever happens is for the highest good and may not manifest exactly as you envision it.

ADDITIONAL SUGGESTIONS:

Find dark and rich dirt or potting soil and carry it. The ultimate grounding! You can also carry a green stone of any kind for balancing your heart chakra. When you feel free of instability, sprinkle the dirt over a growing plant. Send up your thanks for this gift.

∾ INCREASE COMMUNICATION ∾

Communication is the key to relationships. The key to it all is to *hear what is being said*. This is one of the most valuable bits of advice to keep in mind for all interactions. Tell them if you are hurt or what you expect. Sometimes you think they should know or do something—and they don't. Then you get hurt. Meanwhile, you acted as if you were not hurt. Assume that people cannot read your mind. Tell them in a calm, logical way what hurts you or what you expect. It will save you a lot of heartache.

ADVICE:

There, of course, is not one piece of advice but . . . Listen. Don't try to solve or change their feelings. Try to understand the feelings of your loved one. Just listen to them. Feel the problems of your lover—don't solve them. Also, try to inject joy into your communication. Let communicating with you represent pleasure, not pain or obligation. Carve your and your mate's names in the part of the symbol shaped like a house. The arc at the top of the symbol is a beautiful receptacle for spiritual energy and communication.

IDEAL TIMING:

Anytime.

SUGGESTED CANDLE AND GLITTER COLORS:

Yellow of the sun for recognition, joy, and healing. Orange or copper for Mercury.

OILS AND/OR INCENSES:

Goona Goona, Joy and Contentment, Call Me, or Mercury.

MEDITATION:

If new, waxing, or full moon, meditate upon building communication, based upon mutual love and respect. If the moon is waning, send away obstacles to communication. Please say "please" and "thank you" to whomever you believe in and whoever spiritually helps you with your request. Always emphasize that you understand that this is merely a request—a strong request—but you know that whatever happens is for the highest good and may not manifest exactly as you envision it.

ADDITIONAL SUGGESTIONS:

Place Goona Goona oil on your phone (or burn the incense near the phone). Write the name of the person with whom you would like to communicate on paper. Place it under the phone.

Carry a smooth citrine stone in your pocket. When your relationship is on more sure footing, put the stone beside a beautiful tree and send up your thanks for this gift.

~ GET A PERSON TO SIT DOWN AND TALK ABOUT DIFFICULTIES ~

Put your name and the name of your loved one in the large lower circle. Also include astrological signs. You might also need to include the "Emotional Healing" symbol from page 123. Difficulties are a two-way street. Try to honestly examine your wants and agenda, as well as your part in the other person's resistance. Maybe you are being impatient or not letting your needs be known in a way that can be heard without them feeling defensive. Maybe you are sure what you want, but are you sure what you need? Maybe they are not changing the way you want them to, but are you hearing their reasoning? Their resistance may stem from feeling unheard. If they are stressed out or not trusting, use symbols on the candle to address that also. If all else fails, please think about whether this is a good relationship for you.

IDEAL TIMING:
Anytime.

SUGGESTED CANDLE AND GLITTER COLORS:
Blue for peace. Yellow for joy and positive feelings. Orange or copper for the communication of Mercury.

OILS AND/OR INCENSES:
Joy and Contentment, Goona Goona (for building trust and understanding), Love Openness, Clarity, Letting Go, Love Healing, or Indian Bouquet.

MEDITATION:

Envision you and your mate talking and understanding each other. Take it one step further. See the two of you having fun and doing something for relaxation together (not necessarily sex; try something else). Please say "please" and "thank you" to whomever you believe in and whoever spiritually helps you with your request. Always emphasize that you understand that this is merely a request—a strong request—but you know that whatever happens is for the highest good and may not manifest exactly as you envision it.

ADDITIONAL SUGGESTIONS:

Listen. Don't try to solve or change their feelings. Try to understand the feelings of your loved one. Just listen to the problems—don't try to solve them. If they are critical of you, try to understand their point without being defensive. Also, to open channels of communications, emphasize what you like about each other. Lay down rules for fair fighting, if you two tend to get out of control.

∼ GET A RELUCTANT LOVER TO CALL OR SEE YOU ∼

Did you ever have a great time on a date, but they seemed to have forgotten your number? Or have you never been together, but want a person to call you? Try this symbol to get their attention. What happens once they call is up to you—and fate. Keep orange candles burning when you two speak to keep communication clear.

If this is an old relationship, feelings may have to be healed before you can get back together. Use the "Love Healing and Lost Love" symbol on page 71 before using this one. That will heal whatever is keeping you apart, which is essential for *every* love reunion.

To draw this symbol, first draw the bottom section; it is three hearts upside down. Put your lover's name in the top heart and your name along the large curve under it (shaped like an upturned "U").

IDEAL TIMING:

Anytime.

SUGGESTED CANDLE AND GLITTER COLORS:

Yellow of the sun for recognition, joy and healing. Orange or copper for the communication and magnetic qualities of Mercury.

OILS AND/OR INCENSES:

Call Me, Cleopatra, Goona Goona, Spikenard, Fearlessness and Confidence, Love Healing, or Lingering Love.

MEDITATION:

During new, waxing, or full moons, call or beckon this lover to you. There are no guarantees about what they will say, but at least this candle will get them communicating with you so you can see if things can work out. Please say "please" and "thank you" to whomever you believe in and whoever spiritually helps you with your request. Always emphasize that you understand that this is merely a request—a strong request—but you know that whatever happens is for the highest good and may not manifest exactly as you envision it.

ADDITIONAL SUGGESTIONS:

To keep things sweet, sprinkle sugar over your candle. Refer to the "Emotional Healing" symbol on page 125 for additional healing and strength. Place a handful of pure sea salt in your bath. Summon relaxation and strength to trust that the best thing will happen with this love (or someone even better). Envision all blocks to your happiness going down the drain.

Carry a smooth golden stone such as citrine in your pocket. Rub it whenever you feel doubts about love. Repeat to yourself, "The best love will call me and be in my life." You can either keep this stone, as a symbol of your commitment to communicate and to be with a mate who is committed, too, or let it go, as a symbol of letting go of this person in order to let a better, new person into your life.

❧ STOP FIGHTING AND STRESS ❧

This works fabulously for any combination of people who are fighting or not getting along. Use this to heal whatever is wrong between lovers, employees, friends, landlords, enemies, parents, and siblings, etc. You may have to learn to fight fairly and perhaps stop reacting to the way the other reacts. This communication loop forms an endless and hurtful circle, which can eat away at the fibers of a relationship.

IDEAL TIMING:
Anytime.

SUGGESTED CANDLE AND GLITTER COLORS:
Blue causes people to "cool out." It is also for the calming of the deep seas. Silver or white is for the healing of the moon. For dealing with hard-nosed bosses and landlords, use pink. (As weird as that seems, it sweetens up the interactions.)

OILS AND/OR INCENSES:
Healing; Joy and Contentment; Love Healing; Peace, Protection, and Blessings; Coping; Clarity; Stress Reduction; Chamomile; Apple; Anger Be Gone; Cypress (for parent and child); Indian Bouquet; Tuberose; or Kindly Spirit.

MEDITATION:
During new, waxing, and full moons, promote calm, loving feelings and harmony. During waning moons, send away stress. Envision tension and anger between loved ones flowing away. Please say "please" and "thank you" to whomever you believe in and whoever

spiritually helps you with your request. Always emphasize that you understand that this is merely a request—a strong request—but you know that whatever happens is for the highest good and may not manifest exactly as you envision it.

ADDITIONAL SUGGESTIONS:

If someone needs cooling out you can put his or her name on a white taper or a candle shaped like a man or a woman called a "figure" candle. Put the candle into a jar of honey and replace the jar's lid to sweeten your interaction. Place the jar into a pan of water and cover in foil with the shiny side in. Cover with a black plastic bag. Put into freezer and keep it there until you are sure there will be no more trouble.

You can sprinkle the area with Anger Be Gone powder or Basil leaves to dissipate tempers and angry feelings. Envision pain and anger leaving.

~ INCREASE TRUST AND UNDERSTANDING ~

You may wish to increase someone's trust in you. First, can they trust you? Are you being honest—completely honest? Or, do you think they cannot handle the truth? I am referring to daily truth, not a true confession of everything you have done or thought. Living honestly will free you and make your relationship straightforward and easy.

Try to listen. What is your loved one telling you? Does he or she want more time to build trust? Don't rush it. Stop controlling. Enjoy each other. People will trust each other through the other's dependability and reactions. In addition, listening is curative and builds trust.

On the other hand, you may want to open *yourself* up to trust more. Do this symbol with some Love Openness oil and Clarity incense. With this combination, you will make a wise love choice and let down your guard so you can feel and love.

IDEAL TIMING:
Anytime.

SUGGESTED CANDLE AND GLITTER COLORS:
Orange for choices and open doors. Green for growth and love stability. White for purity and openness.

OILS AND/OR INCENSES:
Goona Goona, Clarity, Love Openness, Peach, or Stress Reduction.

MEDITATION:
Meditate upon the blessings coming in at the building or waxing moons. Wane away obstacles at the waning moon. Please say "please" and "thank you" to whomever you believe

in and spiritually helps you with your request. Always emphasize that you understand that this is merely a request—a strong request—but you know that whatever happens is for the highest good and may not manifest exactly as you envision it.

ADDITIONAL SUGGESTIONS:

Put your love's name in the top triangle and your name in the bottom one. If you want to build trust within yourself, write your name in both triangles.

You can also photocopy or hand-copy this seal on parchment or rag bond. Carry it in a little bag with calendula flowers. This will be your talisman to build trust and joy. You can add powdered Goona Goona incense. When you feel free trust, burn the seal, bury the bag and its contents, and send up your thanks for this gift.

∽ SEND A MESSAGE OF LOVE ∽

This is a beautiful symbol to send love to your lover (near or far). It is also a wonderful one to do with your love to affirm your love for each other. Tell your lover what is it for. Notice that there are two sections or lobes. Where they intersect is a symbol of Venus. The two individual lobes form a unified heart. The sign of infinity is at the bottom of the heart. Have your lover carve his or her name in one of the lobes. Put yours in the other. Tell each other what you appreciate about the other. Light this together and seal it with a kiss.

IDEAL TIMING:
Anytime.

SUGGESTED CANDLE AND GLITTER COLORS:
Whichever colors signify your love.

OILS AND/OR INCENSES:
Blessed Light and Thanks, Joy and Contentment, Venus, or Bliss.

MEDITATION:
Send up your thanks for your love. Please say "please" and "thank you" to whomever you believe in and whoever spiritually helps you with your request. Always emphasize that you understand that this is merely a request—a strong request—but you know that whatever happens is for the highest good and may not manifest exactly as you envision it.

ADDITIONAL SUGGESTIONS:

Make it a ritual you share with your loved one. Keep a candle burning for your love. Additional symbols can be added, as necessary. For example, maybe you need more trust, communication, or less stress. Put those symbols on as well. This can be a very strengthening ritual to perform with a love. Psychologically, you are taking time to discuss your relationship. Spiritually, you are sending your wishes and love to the higher realm for blessings.

Make a little bag of personal symbols, small things that mean something to you. Ask your lover to do the same thing. Exchange bags. Then, you can carry a little piece of the other with you at all times. Decide for yourself when it feels good to renew these bags with fresh herbs and items. Carry as long as it feels appropriate for you both and dispose of in a way that feels respectful.

∾ LOVE HEALING AND LOST LOVE ∾

This seal is to heal a relationship, as individuals and as a couple. It also can bring a lost or out-of-touch lover back to you. Be aware this may be manipulative, unless you are pure of heart. You have to sincerely want *to heal* the situation *before* reuniting. Both of you may have done or said hurtful things. You both probably carry some hurt. If you do not heal whatever keeps you apart, you may be able to force a reunion but you will separate again rapidly. Also, be honest with yourself. How much do *they* want reconciliation and how much do *you*? There may be an imbalance that has been brewing for a while.

Your task is to assess what you want and choose an ethical path. If you are tempted to separate someone's relationship it will not work. In magic, whatever you do comes back to you three times, so whatever you do to make them lose the relationship is how you'll lose them, too. Work on your attractiveness, self-esteem, and confidence instead. Try to sincerely heal the hurt between you and another before drawing him or her back to you. Let your lover come back to you because of how great and alluring you are!

After you have sincerely tried to heal the hurt and problems between you (without contacting them, just working spiritually for *healing* only, not reunion) and you have made yourself as attractive and confident as possible—let go and have faith the best thing will happen. They may return, but if they don't, your love was not supposed to be. Perhaps he or she has made a decision for the highest good of all involved and won't come back. Maybe they screwed up what you feel is fate. Maybe they didn't. Either way, we all have choices, even freedom to screw up fate. When you don't get want you want, try to see what you do have and why it all worked out for the best. Additionally, if they did not notice how great you are, they were not right for you. It's a hard process, but go through it now. It is better than knowing too late or spending your life with someone who doesn't really care about you. Carve your name and your lover's name in the circles. Include your astrological signs, if known. If you need support, you can carve a candle for "Letting Go, Transitions, and Passages"; see page 135.

IDEAL TIMING:

New, full, or waning moon.

SUGGESTED CANDLE AND GLITTER COLORS:

Green for healing and deep love.

OILS AND/OR INCENSES:

If the problems were trust, understanding, and communication, use Goona Goona. If the difficulties revolve around enjoying each other, use Joy and Contentment. Overall, Love Healing or Healing oils are the best recommendations.

MEDITATION:

If new or full moon, envision healing what is wrong with the relationship and keeps your lover away. Build and envision a solid and equal relationship. If the moon is waning, see the obstacles that keep you apart fly away. The obstacles may, on the surface, be another person. That is not what you meditate upon. Meditate upon what issues made the other person leave you and choose someone else. If you truly believe someone is holding the person in a relationship against his or her will, do not separate the couple. See your lost lover freed and protected from all manipulation (even yours!). You can only free the person enough so their will is operational again and they can make their own choices. There are no guarantees that once that happens that they will choose you! Please say "please" and "thank you" to whomever you believe in and whoever spiritually helps you with your request. Always emphasize that you understand that this is merely a request—a strong request—but you know that whatever happens is for the highest good and may not manifest exactly as you envision it.

ADDITIONAL SUGGESTIONS:

Throw a handful of sea salt into your bath. As you soak, feel your emotions grounding. Let the water drain out around you. Let go of your fear. Trust and know the best thing will happen for you both.

~ LOVE PROTECTION ~

Sometimes it feels as if our fine relationship is being threatened by outside forces. This seal does not bind a lover to you; it just protects the love and joy you have. Be sure you are not forcing your love or separating the other person from anyone. If these are the situations, read the Ethics section on page 9 and "Love Healing and Lost Love" on page 71.

IDEAL TIMING:
Anytime.

SUGGESTED CANDLE AND GLITTER COLORS:
White for protection and purity. Blue for calming, anger reduction, and protection. Yellow for the joy and light of your love.

OILS AND/OR INCENSES:
Love Protection; Peace, Protection, and Blessings; Joy and Contentment; or Sun.

MEDITATION:
During the new, waxing and full moons, envision a wall of beautiful white light around you and your love. Do not concentrate on whatever could be threatening your love. During the waning moon, envision all threats to your relationship dissolving and fading away. Sometimes we need protection from external forces, such as work or family demands. Don't make these forces dissolve away only for the other person; dissolve how they are negatively impacting your world together. Please say "please" and "thank you" to whomever you believe in and whoever spiritually helps you with your request. Always emphasize that you understand that this is merely a request—a strong request—but you know that whatever happens is for the highest good and may not manifest exactly as you envision it.

ADDITIONAL SUGGESTIONS:

Take a bath filled with white petals and salt. See a globe of white light around you and your love.

Carry a chunk of pure camphor (or a dab of camphor oil) in a little bag with peppermint leaves and rose petals. Add powdered Uncrossing and Protection incenses to the bag if you would like. When you feel free of the need to protect, dissolve the camphor in water, sprinkle the peppermint leaves and rose petals over the earth, keep the bag, and fill it with a treasure (perhaps a gift from your love). Burn the seal and send up your thanks for this gift.

~ GET CLARITY ABOUT A RELATIONSHIP/LOVE CLARITY ~

What's going on? Sometimes we need to know if this is the right love or not. Do they love you? Are you in the relationship for the right reasons?

Sometimes we need to know if we should leave or stay. Is it in your best interest to remain in the relationship? Is their treatment of you temporary and a symptom of something you can work out? Are they telling you to leave?

Are you distracted by a flirtation? Is it an affair or the real thing? Should you leave a partner or forget about having a fling? Should you spend any more time with Mr. or Ms. "Good-Enough-for-Right-Now"? Are you ready for the real thing?

Is your present love on a clear path? What should you do next to preserve the goodness and help it to the next level?

Sometimes we just need a little clarity about how to proceed in a relationship. This is the perfect symbol for shedding light.

IDEAL TIMING:

Waning moon.

SUGGESTED CANDLE AND GLITTER COLORS:

White for all aspects of the issue. Yellow for the sun's power to uncover whatever is hidden. The sun brings things to light and joy.

OILS AND/OR INCENSES:

Love Clarity, Clarity, Sun, Moon, or Mercury.

MEDITATION:

Sit quietly and envision each aspect of the situation. Play out different ways it could be resolved. Measure how comfortable you feel with each resolution. Write down your choices and check off which ones felt the best. It will be interesting for you to see what you feel. Please say "please" and "thank you" to whomever you believe in and whoever spiritually helps you with your request. Always emphasize that you understand that this is merely a request— a strong request—but you know that whatever happens is for the highest good and may not manifest exactly as you envision it.

ADDITIONAL SUGGESTIONS:

Photocopy or hand-copy this seal on parchment or rag bond. Carry it in a little bag with marigold petals (for sun and clarity). When you can see what to do about your love situation, burn the seal bury the bag and its contents, and send up your thanks for this gift.

~ ATTRACTING MARRIAGE ~

First, do you have anyone in mind? If not, carve the "Finding and Attracting the Best Love" symbol on page 45. That symbol can lead you to the right person.

If you do have someone in mind, there are oils available to encourage someone to marry you. Not only are these tools manipulative, what's the point of marrying someone, if they do not want to be with you past the wedding day, or if they make you unhappy?

It's not that you want a marriage; you want a *happy* marriage . . . and it's a process to get there.

Know what you want first. Examine why you are concerned with marriage. Is it a general desire or a symptom of insecurity in the relationship? You do not want someone to marry and love you against his or her will, even if you think you do. You want to be loved *for you*. If you don't believe me, do a gentle pink candle to increase your confidence. If someone is slow to commit, examine the reasons behind the hesitation. Refer to the seals to "Increase Trust," "Increase Communication," "Deepen and Continue a Relationship," "Love Healing," or whatever could be keeping you apart. If someone trusts you and your hurts are healed, the person will feel safe to ask you to marry. Overall, increase the joy between you and if it is the right person, marriage can be the natural progression of your relationship. This symbol will help attract commitment, blessings, fidelity and deep love. Carve your name and sign with your loved one's name and the phrase "or someone even better." Carve into the wax your wishes and be sure to include the phrase "for the highest good of all involved." If you have someone in mind, you don't want to rush things. Rushing and pressure backfire on you. Please do the specific seals to help the situation such as "Love Clarity," "Love Healing," "Increase Communication," or "Eliminate Fear and Insecurity."

IDEAL TIMING:

New moon.

SUGGESTED CANDLE AND GLITTER COLORS:

Gold or yellow for male energy and joy. Silver or white for female energy and purity. Purple for the blessings of divinity.

OILS AND/OR INCENSES:

Gardenia, Orris, Violet, Love Deepening, Myrtle, Orange, or Joy.

MEDITATION:

Pray for the wisdom to know what is your fate in this matter and for the guidance to figure out what is the best thing for you to do. Please say "please" and "thank you" to whomever you believe in and whoever spiritually helps you with your request. Always emphasize that you understand that this is merely a request—a strong request—but you know that whatever happens is for the highest good and may not manifest exactly as you envision it.

ADDITIONAL SUGGESTIONS:

For attracting a proposal, fill a white bowl with pure water. Add a few drops of Gardenia oil. Sleep with this bowl beside the bed. In the morning, pour the water over you in your bath or shower. Continue this until you get your answer of love and marriage (or not). If the other person resists, you may have to heal the relationship in some way. Take one step at a time; marriage is not the first step.

Carry a little bag with rose and lily of the valley petals. You can also include two orris roots and two compatible lodestones. Lodestones are magnetic and should not be carried near your credit cards (because they will strip them). When you have your answer, burn the seal and send up your thanks for this gift.

~ A BLESSING FOR A COUPLE ~

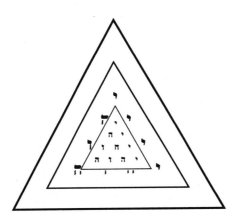

This is a blessing candle for a couple who are marrying, joining together, or "handfasting." There are other symbolic ways to bless the union. Traditionally, brides carry ivy for good and long marriages. For the groom and the bride, a combination of the rose, representing passion, and the lily of the valley, representing purity, is symbolic of a balanced relationship. Also, one of the first things a couple should do for good luck is to plant cabbage in the yard. In urban settings, go buy a potted cabbage together and watch it grow on your windowsill. This symbol contains the great name of God. Please feel free to replace the Hebrew with a blessing from your personal religious framework. This can be for blessing your wedding or someone else's. Be sure to include the names and signs of both parties (if known).

IDEAL TIMING:

Anytime.

SUGGESTED CANDLE AND GLITTER COLORS:

White or silver for the purity of the union and the blessings of female spiritual energy. Yellow or gold for joy, the blessings of the God, and the presence of male energy. Purple for prosperity and the blessings of divinity.

OILS AND/OR INCENSES:

Joy, Gardenia, Pax/Peace/Osiris, Blessing, New Beginnings, Blessed Light and Thanks, or Everything oil.

MEDITATION:

Envision the couple having plenty for all their days. See their love deepening as they grow together. Please say "please" and "thank you" to whomever you believe in and whoever spiritually helps you with your request. Always emphasize that you understand that this is merely a request—a strong request—but you know that whatever happens is for the highest good and may not manifest exactly as you envision it.

ADDITIONAL SUGGESTIONS:

Plant something green for the couple in your own yard or window box. Help it to grow, as you help the couple's relationship to flourish. The tradition of carrying the bride over the threshold (the symbolic divider between worlds) is a great blessing for a new space. It is also the symbol of the beginning of their new life together. Alternately, they can hold hands and walk into their home and over the threshold side by side.

Hand-draw this symbol on a square of rag paper. Place the paper in a white (for love), pink (for romance), or blue (for protection) bag. If blue, this could be the "something blue" for the bride. You could also add rose petals, heather, and lavender to the bag for further blessings and love. Supply the couple with three copper coins. Instruct them to make a wish for each of them individually and the last coin for the relationship. Tell the couple to keep the bag in a treasured spot, as a symbol of their love.

~ OPTIONS IF NO NEW LOVE ARRIVES ~

The act of preparing a candle is your commitment to wanting love or preparing for the perfect love. It states (to whomever you believe in) that you are ready. You are making a spiritual commitment to be open to love. We sometimes don't receive unless we ask. If you started your love candle on the new moon, give it until the full moon to manifest a new flirtation. Nonetheless, you might not have to wait! Once you have focused, the magic is already working. Your love may manifest before you even light it! If nothing happens, be sure you have your eyes open and have not overlooked anyone. Assuming you haven't, repeat the previous procedure. The candle can be preparing you for love. Sometimes our soul mate is not ready to arrive within the time your candle burns.

There may be obstacles within you. You may not be mentally ready yet. You may need to feel more open and explore what bringing in a lover might mean to you and your way of life. Examine why having a love is so important—or unimportant. We do not have to be transcended masters to meet our true loves; we just have to have the right energy. Remember what it's like to be the new person in town or at a job? There is a fresh energy, a glow, and a light. Try to bring that energy into yourself. Clear yourself of negativity and self-doubt. With that energy, the best love will be drawn to you. (And even if you can't clear negativity and self-doubt, you can still find love . . . read on.)

The following addresses what may be obstacles to finding love and how to conquer them. Obstacles may be:

~ a need for general clearing (to start with new freshness) Use "Love Uncrossing and Clearing," which clears past mucky relationships and problems in a present relationship.

~ mental blocks, so carve a candle using "Eliminating Mental Blocks to Love"; see page 84.

~ inability to release and let go of love, so carve "Letting Go of Old or Present Love"; see page 86.

~ LOVE UNCROSSING AND CLEARING ~

This seal is good for *past and present* tumultuous relationships, which are confusing or interfering in having good love—directly, indirectly, psychically, or mentally. It can also help you let go of love that is not in your best interest. This symbol gets rid of negativity and blocks surrounding your path to true love. "Uncrossing" means eliminating whatever "crosses" your path, which is in the way of your highest progress. Of course, if a lover is interfering with you physically or you are in danger, please contact the police and see Part VII, Clearing, Protection, and Justice, page 181). If you are clearing the way for good love, carve your name and astrological sign into the candle wax. If you are clearing miscommunications and "bad vibes" around your relationship, include both your names and astrological signs. Do not include the names of anyone who is creating negativity. The blessings come to the names on the candle.

IDEAL TIMING:
Waning moon or when necessary.

SUGGESTED CANDLE OR GLITTER COLORS:
Gold or yellow for the sun. Silver or white for emotional healing. White or pink also can be used for purity and sweet love.

OILS AND/OR INCENSES:
Love Uncrossing; Uncrossing; Letting Go; Banishing; Joy and Contentment; Purification and Rejuvenation; Sun; Moon; Peace, Protection, and Blessings; Frankincense; Myrrh; Rue; or Healing.

MEDITATION:

Meditate upon sending away past and present obstacles (physical and mental) to meeting your new love or correcting the problems of your present relationship. Feel the problems and blocks flowing easily off of you. Let them go. Envision light and love around you. Please say "please" and "thank you" to whomever you believe in and whoever spiritually helps you with your request. Always emphasize that you understand that this is merely a request—a strong request—but you know that whatever happens is for the highest good and may not manifest exactly as you envision it.

ADDITIONAL SUGGESTIONS:

Draw a bath and sprinkle white rose petals or petals from a white flower that feels right for clearing any blocks to your love. Envision your wish coming true for the highest good of everyone involved. Let the water drain out around you. Feel the obstacles and blocks leave you as the water does.

Photocopy or hand-copy this seal on parchment or rag bond. Carry it with cloves and peppermint leaves in a little bag. This should be your talisman to stop the interference, problems, and negativity, and to mend any hurt. When you feel free of any problems or negativity in love, burn the seal and send up your thanks for this gift.

~ ELIMINATING MENTAL BLOCKS TO LOVE ~

This symbol is great for preparing you for love. If you have mental blocks and doubts about starting a new relationship, carve the symbol below on a candle. Inscribe your name and astrological sign on the horizontal arm of the seal.

IDEAL TIMING:

Waning moon or when necessary.

SUGGESTED CANDLE AND GLITTER COLORS:

Gold or yellow for the sun. Silver or white for emotional healing. White or pink also can be used for purity and openness to love.

OILS AND/OR INCENSES:

Love Clarity; Clarity; Letting Go; Coping; Rose; Frankincense; Moon; Peace, Protection, and Blessings; or Healing.

MEDITATION:

Meditate upon sending away past and present mental obstacles to bringing in the best love to you. Pray to be shown the blocks and watch them dissolve. Become clear about what kind of relationship you want. Also become clear about what your fears are about starting anew and how to overcome them. Please say "please" and "thank you" to whomever you believe in and whoever spiritually helps you with your request. Always emphasize that you understand that this is merely a request—a strong request—but you know that whatever happens is for the highest good and may not manifest exactly as you envision it.

ADDITIONAL SUGGESTIONS:

Meditate upon uncovering your blocks. Once you have identified and named them, write them down as a list. Go to your sink with the list and a box of sugar cubes (one cube for each block). Hold a cube and name it after one of your blocks. Say the name of the block aloud, and pour water on the cube. Watch it dissolve as you feel lighter and free of the blocks. If you are feeling blocked even about this procedure, you may want to talk to a friend or a mental health professional to help you get clarity at this time.

Photocopy or hand-copy this seal on parchment or rag bond. Carry it in a little bag with frankincense, lavender, and balm of Gilead. This should be your talisman to stop mental blocks and mend your heart. When you feel free of your blocks, burn the seal and send up your thanks for this gift.

～ LETTING GO OF OLD OR PRESENT LOVE ～

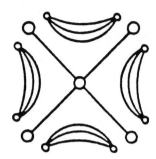

Old Love: Sometimes there is no room for new love, because in your heart and mind, a past love is ever present. Although you may not see each other, you are having trouble letting go. You may imagine that there is still hope for you two. Let go of the hope, as scary as that sounds. Your life can open, then, to an even better match.

Present Love: You may know, logically, that this relationship isn't or wasn't right, but your heart doesn't follow. Even though it hurts, it may be time to let go.

～ Don't be afraid to stop waiting and continue living. If you don't, you may resent the person.

～ Real relationships are equal partnerships; he or she must make time for you, too.

～ You do not have to wait for someone who is not currently meeting your needs. Keep walking in your journey. If they are is the right person, they will catch up to you, even if you have "closed" some emotions. When and if they catch up, you will be able to assess the relationship more clearly since, in the meantime, you have had other experiences. Waiting can be part of a relationship, but, give yourself a deadline. If they do not contact you within a reasonable time, move on. Let fate have some room to bring someone even better into your life.

Place your name and zodiac sign in the center circle of this symbol. Also see the "Confidence and Self-esteem" seal on page 113.

Good-bye is a contraction of "God be with you." Send them away with blessings.

IDEAL TIMING:

Waning moon or when necessary.

SUGGESTED CANDLE AND GLITTER COLORS

Gold or yellow for the sun. Silver or white for purity and emotional healing. Pink can be used for affection and attracting love.

OILS AND/OR INCENSES:

Letting Go, Love Healing, Clarity, Cypress, Sun, Joy and Contentment, or Balm of Gilead.

MEDITATION:

To send away past and present obstacles (physical and mental) to meeting your new love, let go of the old person. Envision them receding into the haze. Then, see the new love running toward you. Do this exercise until you can see the old lover no more and the new one becomes clear. Our mind plays tricks and may make the person running toward you have the face of the old lover (instead of the new). If this is the case, let the old lover run toward you and completely miss you. Let them keep running. Repeat until you see a new love that feels fresh and makes you revitalized. Please say "please" and "thank you" to whomever you believe in and whoever spiritually helps you with your request. Always emphasize that you understand that this is merely a request—a strong request—but you know that whatever happens is for the highest good and may not manifest exactly as you envision it.

ADDITIONAL SUGGESTIONS:

As a releasing ritual, write the name of the person you would like to let go of on a piece of parchment or rag paper. Burn it to let them go. Say aloud, "I release you for the highest good. I release myself for the highest good. Thank you." You can also wash that man (or woman) right out of your hair! Put some of your shampoo in your palm. Add a few drops of Letting Go oil and wash your hair as usual. Let the person go as the soap travels down the drain.

PART IV

SEX AND PASSION

S ex can be one of the greatest healers or one of the most devastating destroyers. Either way, sex is communication. As with sex, sex magic must be mutual. In this way, sex should never be forced. These suggestions should be used with a current lover who willingly consents to make love to you. Candles for sex and passion can be done without your partner's knowledge, but watch out. Interfering and having your partner's inhibitions suddenly be released can be confusing to the partner and may backfire on you. The best way is to have a consenting partner. Mutual consent and passion enhances the process. By not sharing this Candle Therapy with your lover, you miss out on sex magic's true power. If you are tempted to move a relationship into the sexual arena before its time (either through candles or force), you will lose. If you are anxious to bed down a reluctant partner, refer to the Ethics section in Part I, page 9. Nothing in magic and life should be forced.

C. F. Riggs-Bergesen

~ OVERCOME OBSTACLES TO GREAT SEX ~

Are you scared your lover will mock you or not understand if you try this candle? Try it! Tell your lover that this candle is going to make you both have the best sex you have ever had. The suggestion alone, of course, is overwhelming and empowering. Therefore, for maximum effect, have your lover carve his or her name on the candle after you have finished carving the seal. Explain the symbols in a sexy way. Both of you can participate in oiling it as well. (*But use gloves or wash your hands before diving into sex*—the oils can irritate and are not to be taken internally. Be careful not to rub your eyes or other membranes!)

Do candles to increase communication or heal whatever obstacles are in the way to love, instead of being pushy. There's nothing sexier than someone who wants you.

P.S. And there's nothing sexier than making safe-sex sexy!

IDEAL TIMING:
Anytime.

SUGGESTED CANDLE AND GLITTER COLORS:
Red for passion. Silver or white for feminine energy. Gold or yellow for male energy. Orange for overcoming obstacles to this communication. Purple for blessings of the divine.

OILS AND/OR INCENSES:
Voodoo Nights Sex, Khus Khus, Love Intoxication, Strawberry, or Glamour and Seduction.

MEDITATION:
Sit in a bathtub before your encounter and envision the most fabulous and amazing sex you have ever had with your partner. If he or she is participating, have them fantasize as you light the candle and start touching each other. Please say "please" and "thank you" to

whomever you believe in and whoever spiritually helps you with your request. Always emphasize that you understand that this is merely a request—a strong request—but you know that whatever happens is for the highest good and may not manifest exactly as you envision it.

ADDITIONAL SUGGESTIONS:

For the best sex ever, write "great sex" or something similar on a red candle. Also write your name and your sex partner's name and "for the highest mutual good and enjoyment"— and enjoy. As mentioned above, it makes it even better when you include your lover in the process. Remember, this is not to manipulate someone into having sex, but to enhance the joy or overcome any blocks you and your lover may have.

∾ OVERCOME IMPOTENCE ∾

Physical difficulties, such as discomfort or impotence, may indicate the presence of a medical condition, which should be determined by a physician. Also, certain medications inhibit sexual desire and physical ability to gain erection or orgasm. Many medications act upon neurotransmitters and other chemical systems, producing these side effects. Once you have considered the medical possibilities, consider candles. *If this is done for another person, please get their permission.* Include both your names and astrological signs on the candle.

IDEAL TIMING:
Anytime.

SUGGESTED CANDLE AND GLITTER COLORS:
Red for strength and lust. Silver or white for female energy. Gold or yellow for male energy.

OILS AND/OR INCENSES:
Voodoo Nights Sex, Frankincense, or Deer's-tongue (herb or oil).

MEDITATION:
Envision the person strong and free of impotence and fears. At new or full moon, build sexual stamina and confidence. During the waning moon, send impotence away. Please say "please" and "thank you" to whomever you believe in and whoever spiritually helps you with your request. Always emphasize that you understand that this is merely a request—a strong request—but you know that whatever happens is for the highest good and may not manifest exactly as you envision it.

ADDITIONAL SUGGESTIONS:

Hand-copy this symbol on a piece of paper. Carry it in a little bag. When you or the other person feel free of impotence, burn the seal and send up your thanks for this gift.

~ GET RID OF INHIBITIONS ~

This is a great symbol to use for experiencing your true sexual potential. About removing inhibitions, be sure to read the Ethics section on page 9 and the information from the "Overcome Obstacles to Great Sex" seal on page 90. Be careful not to force an issue without a person's knowledge. One of the many reasons not to do this without permission is that the release of inhibitions can scare the other person and severely deteriorate trust. They could feel swept away by your agenda, not their own willing release. Do not do this for selfish reasons. The person or both people in a couple who need this should do this personally.

IDEAL TIMING:
New, full, or waning moon.

SUGGESTED CANDLE AND GLITTER COLORS:
Red for lust and passion.

OILS AND/OR INCENSES:
VaVoom, Voodoo Nights Sex, Frankincense, Narcissus, Aphrodisiac Blend, Lime, or Narcissus.

MEDITATION:
In the new or full moon, build sexual freedom, enjoyment, and confidence. In the waning moon, send inhibitions away. Please say "please" and "thank you" to whomever you believe in and whoever spiritually helps you with your request. Always emphasize that you understand that this is merely a request—a strong request—but you know that whatever happens is for the highest good and may not manifest exactly as you envision it.

ADDITIONAL SUGGESTIONS:

Photocopy or hand-copy this symbol onto parchment or rag bond. You can carry it in a little bag. When you or the person feels free of inhibitions, burn the seal, bury the bag, and send up thanks for this gift.

～ MAKE YOURSELF
SEXUALLY IRRESISTIBLE ～

Put your name and astrological sign on any kind of candle to make yourself irresistible. Anoint the candle with one of the oils listed below to make you the hottest number ever!

If you are new to this relationship and you want it to last and build, I have an aside. One of the hardest decisions my friends have is when is the right time to have sex in the relationship. After such an intense energy exchange as sex, it's going to be confusing if you haven't built a solid friendship first. You might want to try the "Making Yourself More Attractive and Irresistible" symbol in Part III, Love, instead of this one; see page 47. Be irresistible, glamorous, seductive, and mysterious!

IDEAL TIMING:
Anytime.

SUGGESTED CANDLE AND GLITTER COLORS:
Red for lust and passion.

OILS AND/OR INCENSES:
Come to Me, Irresistibility, Glamour and Seduction, Dixie Love, VaVoom, Khus Khus, Queen, Mysterious, Love Intoxication, or Cleopatra.

MEDITATION:
See yourself attracting as many love partners as you can imagine, but see them as great choices. Envision how much they desire you, but be sure to envision fun, safe, and manageable attraction. Specify in your mind the kind of people you would like to attract. Revel in the feeling. If you have one in mind, see his or her face. Get ready for a delicious evening.

Please say "please" and "thank you" to whomever you believe in and whoever spiritually helps you with your request. Always emphasize that you understand that this is merely a request—a strong request—but you know that whatever happens is for the highest good and may not manifest exactly as you envision it.

ADDITIONAL SUGGESTIONS:

Hand-copy this seal onto a piece of beautiful paper. Carry it in a little bag. When you feel irresistible and burn the seal, you can bury the bag or fill it full of sweet candies to eat when you want to feel sweet. Send up your thanks for this gift.

~ INCREASE INTIMACY
DURING LOVEMAKING ~

Sexual relations may be wonderful between you, but sometimes you can be left wondering if the other person is really present in the experience. Or maybe it seems passionate enough, but is too fast and impersonal. Burn any candles, but figure candles are especially appropriate for this work. While making love, use pink, white, or green figure candles to represent you and your partner. Let them melt and merge into one. Assess if there are other issues going on that could be hampering your intimacy, such as communication and trust difficulties. Add those symbols from Part III, Love, on the candle at the same time.

IDEAL TIMING:
Anytime.

SUGGESTED CANDLE AND GLITTER COLORS:
Red for lusty intimacy. White for purity, sensitivity, and healing. Pink for sweetness and romance. Green for love deepening and growth.

OILS AND/OR INCENSES:
Spiritual Sex, Goona Goona, Venus, Jasmine Rose, or Gardenia.

MEDITATION:
In the full and building moon, envision a strengthening and opening of your love. In the waning moon, let obstacles to the intimacy wane away. See them slowly and softly traveling down a drain. Please say "please" and "thank you" to whomever you believe in and whoever spiritually helps you with your request. Always emphasize that you understand that this is

merely a request—a strong request—but you know that whatever happens is for the highest good and may not manifest exactly as you envision it.

ADDITIONAL SUGGESTIONS:

Before making love, feel relaxed and solid about yourself and your lover. Tell your lover that you would like tonight to be a time during which all sensation will be felt. Ideally, the pace needs to be slow and loving. Take note of how things feel. If your lover has a tendency to space out or fantasize while in bed with you, ask him or her to remain with you during the experience of making love. Look at each other and sometimes talk (not like a porno movie; like lovers).

Photocopy or hand-copy the above seal on parchment or rag bond. Carry the symbol in a little bag. Place it near the candle or under the mattress. When you feel intimacy is part of your love, burn the seal and send up your thanks for this gift. If necessary, copy the seal again when you have a new lover. Use one seal per lover.

≈ GETTING PREGNANT ≈

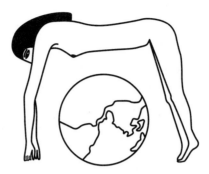

Most religions embrace the symbology of birth, continuum, and rebirth. As most couples who have had a child can affirm, pregnancy is a spiritual act. Getting pregnant involves timing, health, and a spiritual blessing. Include your name and astrological sign on the candle. Keep your mate very involved in this process. Have the person inscribe their name and sign on the candle as well. You can wish aloud on three pennies each and place the six pennies around the base of the candle. Light the candle together. Let your two matches merge to one.

IDEAL TIMING:
Anytime, especially on the new moon.

SUGGESTED CANDLE AND GLITTER COLORS:
Silver or white for the moon. Green for growth and Venus energy.

OILS AND/OR INCENSES:
Wish Fulfillment, Myrtle, Orange, Patchouli, Hazel, Watermelon, Cyclamen, Cucumber, Pine, or Isis. Be sure to use gloves when handling any oils, herbs, or incenses while pregnant.

MEDITATION:
At new, full, or waxing moons, see yourself becoming full with child. At waning moons, send obstacles to getting pregnant far away. Please say "please" and "thank you" to whomever you believe in and whoever spiritually helps you with your request. Always emphasize that you understand that this is merely a request—a strong request—but you know that whatever happens is for the highest good and may not manifest exactly as you envision it.

ADDITIONAL SUGGESTIONS:
To help things along, place fresh daffodils around the bedroom to increase fertility. Coriander seeds strewn around the room stimulate the creation of a unique and creative child.

Also, you can eat pomegranate, mustard, or cucumber seeds to promote conception. Please consult a physician before taking anything internally.

Photocopy or hand-copy this seal on parchment or rag bond. Carry it in a little bag with mistletoe, mugwort, an acorn, or a pinecone to aid in conception. Add powdered Venus and Protection incenses. When you get pregnant, make an offering (do a good deed, for example), burn the seal, and send up your thanks for this amazing gift. Keep the little bag as part of your child's first experiences and attach it to their "baby book," if you have one.

~ STAYING PREGNANT ~

Please go to the doctor and/or midwife regularly. No drinking, smoking, or drugs. Please eat well, pray, and follow all prenatal advice. Also, keep symbols of fertility around you, such as Hecate, a dark goddess (who is sometimes represented as a frog). She presides over conception and birth. She was present when the Egyptian goddess, Isis, goddess of love, creation, and rebirth, resuscitated her dead husband, Osiris.

IDEAL TIMING:

Anytime.

SUGGESTED CANDLE AND GLITTER COLORS:

Blue for the safety of the ocean and peace. White for all aspects being good and protected. Green for the blessings of Venus.

OILS AND/OR INCENSES:

Strong Protection; Stress Reduction; Pax/Peace/Osiris; or Peace, Protection, and Blessings. Be sure to use gloves when handling any oils, herbs, or incenses while pregnant.

MEDITATION:

If waxing, full, or new moons, build your strength and feel your child grow and thrive inside of you. If waning moon, send all obstacles away that threaten you and your child's health. Please say "please" and "thank you" to whomever you believe in and whoever spiritually helps you with your request. Always emphasize that you understand that this is merely a request—a strong request—but you know that whatever happens is for the highest good and may not manifest exactly as you envision it.

ADDITIONAL SUGGESTIONS:

You can carry strawberry leaves in a little green bag to ease pregnancy pain. Also get some snapdragons, a protective flower, for your bedroom.

The seal for the candle is based upon labyrinths, which are ancient symbols of fertility, safety, and wisdom. Labyrinthine structures are found repeatedly in our lives. For example, this view from a four-story walk-up brownstone in New York City is a modern labyrinth. As reinforcement to this magic, become more aware of the labyrinths you encounter daily. When you notice one, silently reaffirm your desire to stay pregnant and safely deliver your child.

~ SAFE BIRTH AND DELIVERY ~

Safety is of the utmost importance. Certainly, for a safe birth, merging the advances of Western medicine with the truths and wisdom of the old ways is ideal.

IDEAL TIMING:

Anytime.

SUGGESTED CANDLE AND GLITTER COLORS:

White for protection, purity, and the most powerful help for your request.

OILS AND/OR INCENSES:

Cyclamen for safe passages and Rosemary for smooth labor. You can also use Hyacinth; Wish Fulfillment; Stress Reduction; Isis; Peace, Protection, and Blessings; Fearlessness and Confidence; or Joy and Contentment. Be sure to use gloves when handling any oils, herbs, or incenses while pregnant.

MEDITATION:

If waxing, new, or full moons, see light filling you. Envision the ease of the birth. Feel your new life resting in your arms. Feel relaxation and strength bathe you. In the waning moon, send away all fear, complications, and doubt. Please say "please" and "thank you" to whomever you believe in and whoever spiritually helps you with your request. Always emphasize that you understand that this is merely a request—a strong request—but you know that whatever happens is for the highest good and may not manifest exactly as you envision it.

ADDITIONAL SUGGESTIONS:

Try to let the candle remain burning while you are in the delivery room. Read the After a Birth section, page 106.

Photocopy this seal and handwrite your name and more of the loved ones who will be present or are sending love to you. Put it in a little cloth bag and bring it to the delivery. After your wonderful delivery, burn the seal and send up your thanks for this gift.

~ AFTER A BIRTH ~

I hope your birthing was (or will be) a wonderful and safe experience. Even if all did not proceed as planned or if this pregnancy was in some way terminated, your body was still pregnant. There are definite aftercare steps to be taken. Your body is trying to return to its natural balance.

In addition, postpartum depression may be very severe in some women. It is especially severe in women who have PMS (PMT in the United Kingdom). PMS or Premenstrual Syndrome, affects almost 50 percent of all women and usually goes untreated. It is caused by a lack of the hormone progesterone and its interaction with estrogen at various points in your cycle. In pregnancy, a woman has, at times, multiples of the prepregnancy levels of progesterone. When the baby is delivered, women with PMS experience the drop in progesterone as a major crash.

PMS can ruin the lives and relationships of those women with it. It is ironic that it is so often overlooked, because its cyclical nature makes it easy to diagnose. Although symptoms are quite individual and varied, they usually occur from the time of ovulation to the onset of menses. For at least three months, chart your symptoms such as weeping, depression, irritability, bloating, weight gain, cravings, headaches, etc. Can you see a pattern? Treatment can be straightforward with a regimen of exercise, vitamins, and/or natural progesterone supplements. England has had excellent treatment of this disorder for more than fifty years. For many sociological and economic reasons, this treatment has not been available to American women. In America, most physicians still prescribe tranquilizers and antidepressants alone. These are helpful but often incomplete treatments. In addition, use of the pill can be dangerous and *synthetic* progesterone can aggravate PMS. These will make you worse if you have PMS. As an aside, you might need natural progesterone *and* another treatment involving tranquilizers, antidepressants, and vitamins.

There are only a few pharmacies that carry *natural* progesterone. The original in this country is Madison Pharmacy (800-558-7046, 608-833-7046). They are a reputable organization with a solid history of helping women. They conduct research and are contributing daily to the betterment of women's lives throughout the country. Ask them for a referral to a physician who can manage your progesterone treatment and prescriptions in your area. *Beware* of groups calling themselves PMS treatment centers, which do not use natural progesterone. A major medical center and hospital in New York City has a large research grant for PMS study. In this program (run by women), it is stated that lack of natural progesterone is not the cause of PMS and the participants are given antidepressants and tranquilizers only. Beware! Again, please contact Madison Pharmacy for referrals leading to the proper treatment. PMS is not something made up—a catch phrase to keep women down—it is a physical imbalance of progesterone. It is debilitating if left untreated.

~ OILS FOR LOVE, SEX, AND PREGNANCY ~

Please check the Appendix, page 204, for more extensive explanations.

AMBERGRIS is used for sensual attraction, as are other smells from animals.

ANGER BE GONE helps one let go of pent-up anger, annoyances, and hostile feelings.

APHRODISIAC BLEND (or also called Aphrodisiac Potion) inspires lust and passion.

APPLE brings friends, peace of mind, relaxation, and successful projects.

ATTRACT SOUL MATE ROMANCE attracts the highest love to you.

ATTRACTION can attract and find anything for you.

BALM OF GILEAD helps you let go, heals a broken heart, and eases the pain of loss.

BANISHING removes all negativity, bad influences, spirits, and even lingering roommates.

BASIL creates harmony and disarms disagreements.

BAY uncrosses, protects, and harmonizes opposites.

BLESSINGS can be used to bless any relationship and bring good things.

BLESSED LIGHT AND THANKS is for giving thanks and acknowledging your plenty.

BLISS brings exquisite bliss and joy! Great for beating the blues!

CALL ME does just what it says! It gets someone to call for business or pleasure.

CAMELLIA is great for personal growth and self-confidence.

CAMPHOR brings clarity and purity to a situation.

CARDAMON attracts love and gives a sexy spice to situations.

CHAMOMILE is good for purification and unhexing. Very, very, very relaxing.

CIVET is used in musky blends for lusty attraction. Use only one-half to one drop because of its unpleasant scent.

CLARITY increases focus, mental clarity, and concentration. Great for making decisions.

CLEOPATRA is one of the most powerful ancient formulae for attraction and seduction.

COME TO ME does what it says and is pushy about it. Use with caution.

COPING brings the ability to deal with the situations at hand and whatever is thrown at you.

COURTING produces people to court you or changes what you have into a courting situation.

CUCUMBER is used for healing and to instill fertility. You can eat the seeds from a fresh cucumber, too!

CYCLAMEN is for safe passage and all kinds of transitions.

CYPRESS eases grief, worry, and loss.

DAMIANA is a powerful aphrodisiac.

DEER'S-TONGUE awakens lust and is a strong attraction and anti-impotence herb.

DIXIE LOVE is an old Southern blend that makes you irresistible.

EVERYTHING brings it all. Concentrate on what "everything" means to you. Be as specific as possible.

FAITH is essential for relaxing in love and knowing the best love will come your way.

FEARLESSNESS AND CONFIDENCE conquers fears and insecurities. Pushes projects forward.

FRANGIPANI fosters joie de vivre, love, trust, and friendships. Flirty.

FRANKINCENSE is for protection, prosperity, success, acclaim, health, and clarity.

GARDENIA strengthens commitments. A classic marriage and true love flower.

GINGER is used to attract love, money, courage, love, and sex.

GLAMOUR AND SEDUCTION makes one fabulous and alluring. Very passionate.

GLITZ, FUN, AND LUST is one of our most popular blends. Have fun!

GOONA GOONA fosters trust, communication, and understanding. Eases relationship problems.

HAZEL gives wisdom and fertility.

HEALING attunes one to vibrations to heal the body and mind.

HYACINTH is good for relaxing, easing the pain of childbirth, and erasing nightmares.

INDIAN BOUQUET brings harmony to warring couples. Brings peace and understanding.

IRRESISTIBILITY makes you irresistible and tasty smelling. For business or pleasure.

ISIS was created for the Egyptian goddess of love, rebirth, and creation.

JASMINE is both sensual and spiritual.

JOY AND CONTENTMENT injects the daily jolt of joy and empowerment you need. Banishes depression.

KHUS KHUS is an old Southern blend that makes you irresistible to the opposite sex.

KINDLY SPIRIT makes people like you and be sympathetic to your cause.

LAVENDER brings true and respectful love. A wonderful antidepressant.

LETTING GO helps one to let go gently and completely. Good for bringing in the new.

LILAC brings peace and harmony, as well as attracting fun love.

LILY OF THE VALLEY is for pure love! Balances the passion of rose.

LIME can release inhibitions. Very sexual and intense.

LINGERING LOVE is a romantic oil that keeps you on the mind of your loved one.

LONG-LASTING LOVE attracts love for potential long-term, soul mate level relationships.

LOVE CLARITY brings clarity to you and your loved one about the relationship.

LOVE DEEPENING deepens your ongoing relationship to the next level. But don't force it!

LOVE HEALING heals a relationship so you can continue or reunite.

LOVE INTOXICATION is great for enhancing attraction and sprucing up your current love.

LOVE OPENNESS opens you and another up to love.

LOVE POTION 131 attracts the best love to you for this time in your life.

LOVE PROTECTION protects the love you have from external forces.

LOVE UNCROSSING removes negativity that could be keeping you and a lover apart.

MARJORAM keeps loyalty around you. Strengthens love and joy.

MARS AND MOTIVATION brings strength, fearlessness, and confidence.

MERCURY enhances communication and opens the doors to connections and opportunities.

MOON is a wonderful healing blend for worshipping the moon goddess and healing.

MUSK is one of the most popular ingredients in sex blends. Brings willpower and determination.

MYRRH purifies space and consecrates objects.

MYSTERIOUS makes you alluring and mysterious.

MYRTLE promotes love, fidelity, and fertility.

NARCISSUS gives confidence, strength, self-love, fearlessness, and will.

NEROLI is a classic love, as well as wealth-attraction, scent.

NEW BEGINNINGS brings about new starts in general or specific areas of life.

NUTMEG eliminates negativity.

ORANGE is a solar scent and a classic for courting and love. Also for good luck.

ORRIS is used for attracting deep love and commitment.

PATCHOULI is great for lust, money, power, fertility, and grounding.

PAX/PEACE/OSIRIS creates an atmosphere of perpetual protection and peace in a relationship.

PEACE, PROTECTION, AND BLESSINGS (also called Protection) brings all three! A powerful shield of light.

PEACH is used for creating an atmosphere of respect and decorum. Attracts love and fertility.

PEPPERMINT protects and brings luck. Don't wear it directly on the skin; it's very irritating.

PINE brings blessings and fertility. Cleanses.

PURIFICATION AND REJUVENATION purifies and brings new life.

QUEEN is used by women to attract men for passion.

ROSE brings love, devotion, sex, beauty, and peace.

ROSEMARY is good for easing labor in childbirth and resolving problems, too.

RUE is a strong protector. Helps one to let go of unrequited love.

SPIKENARD brings stability and fidelity to a relationship or situation.

SPIRITUAL SEX is used for experiencing sex on a spiritual level (with and without a partner).

STRAWBERRY is powerfully sexual, lusty, and passionate.

STRESS REDUCTION reduces the stress, tension, and fighting.

STRONG PROTECTION is for the strongest protection. Good to allay fears and in emergencies.

SUN brings health, wealth, happiness, healing, joy, fame, and success.

TUBEROSE relaxes and sends peace. Attracts secure and peaceful love relationships.

UNCROSSING unhexes and eliminates all negativity and bad vibrations.

VANILLA brings everything from love to success. Wear it to be alluring and fabulous.

VAVOOM is for big-time sex appeal and flair. Be the most *faaabulous* you can be!

VENUS is not only a devotional oil for the goddess Venus, but a classic rose-based love scent.

VERBENA is used to enhance attractiveness.

VIOLET is a love scent that brings high respect and depth.

VOODOO NIGHTS SEX is luscious and sexy. Enhances your sex life, especially with a loved one.

WATERMELON is for fertility, pregnancy, and plenty. It's a great seduction oil, too.

WISH FULFILLMENT brings your wish, but be very focused on one clear and ethical wish. Be careful for what you wish.

YLANG YLANG makes one attractive, impressive, and expressive.

◆

PART V

PERSONAL GROWTH AND HEALING

Since externals are often more obviously demanding, it is sometimes difficult to focus on our internal process. Nonetheless, our personal growth, or lack thereof, is the filter through which the externals travel. It is highly recommended to add the following symbols to any of your other magical work.

Personal growth is one of the most important aspects of all therapy . . . and life. Actually, personal growth and therapy are almost synonymous, since in all areas of one's life, elements of confidence, happiness, and spirituality come into play.

Healing is another aspect of growth. Although there are separate seals for emotional and physical healing, the mind and body are not separate. There can be no physical healing without emotional healing and vice versa. Your meditations, however, should focus upon what is the predominant issue at hand. It may vary from time to time during the course of an illness or disease.

The priority in physical healing is to seek medical attention for yourself or your loved one. Avail yourself of everything that Western *and* alternative therapies have to offer. Use what works. After (and while) pursuing medical care, one can burn candles for many aspects of healing. Healings should always be done with the consent of the ill person. If the person is in pain, meditate upon freeing the person from discomfort. If a person is too ill to consent and you feel a healing is necessary, do it, but take heed: Be sure to include in your prayer that *you* think healing is necessary and will be grateful for whatever form in which the healing comes. Thank whoever, spiritually, would affect the healing. One should not overlook the fact that fate may hold a different plan for this person than what you think should happen. Even pain is sometimes necessary. It can spur a person to seek long-avoided medical attention. And, sadly for us left behind, death is sometimes a healing, too. Be open to whatever form in which healing manifests.

❧ CONFIDENCE AND SELF-ESTEEM ❧

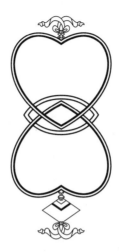

Confidence involves removing fear and increasing self-esteem. To increase self-esteem, self-love is the main ingredient. You can add the symbols for "Happiness and Joy," "Elimination of fear," and "A Blast of Sunlight and Energy," as appropriate. You may also want to read the section ahead on Emotional Healing and the section on PMS in After a Birth, on page 106.

Put your name in both hearts. In the top heart, write your name. Then reverse the candle and write your name in the bottom heart (so that it is upside down when you sit the candle upright again). Your name will then be a mirror reflection. Your names will face each other. This is a symbol of love and thereby, you will fall in love with yourself.

IDEAL TIMING:
Anytime.

SUGGESTED CANDLE AND GLITTER COLORS:
Yellow or gold for warmth, healing, and confidence, and healing of the sun. Pink for loving yourself. Green for growth and healing.

OILS AND/OR INCENSES:
Fearlessness and Confidence, Sun, or Seven African Powers.

MEDITATION:
If it is a new moon, meditate upon building self-confidence, security, and self-love. If it is a full moon, light the candle feeling fearless and confident. If the moon is waning, send away feelings of self-doubt, fear of judgment, or nervousness. Please say "please" and "thank

you" to whomever you believe in and whoever spiritually helps you with your request. Always emphasize that you understand that this is merely a request—a strong request—but you know that whatever happens is for the highest good and may not manifest exactly as you envision it.

ADDITIONAL SUGGESTIONS:

Photocopy or hand-copy this seal on parchment or rag bond. Give an offering that means something to you. You can carry the seal in a little bag. When you feel confident and proud, burn the seal, bury the bag, and send up your thanks for this gift.

~ ELIMINATION OF FEAR ~

This is for the elimination of fear, self-doubt, and worry. This symbol covers all areas of life. In Part III, Love, there is a specific symbol "Eliminate Fear and Insecurity"; see page 51. Choose which one fits best.

IDEAL TIMING:

Anytime.

SUGGESTED CANDLE AND GLITTER COLORS:

Red for fearlessness and courage at waxing moons. At the waning moon, use blue for relaxing in the face of fear.

OILS AND/OR INCENSES:

Mars and Motivation, Balm of Gilead, Camellia (alone or mixed with Venus oil), or Fearlessness and Confidence. To push an art or business project forward, use Success Blast. If it feels impossible, use Saint Jude.

MEDITATION:

At the waxing moon, build courage and confidence. At the waning moon, send away fear and eliminate it. Please say "please" and "thank you" to whomever you believe in and whoever spiritually helps you with your request. Always emphasize that you understand that this is merely a request—a strong request—but you know that whatever happens is for the highest good and may not manifest exactly as you envision it.

ADDITIONAL SUGGESTIONS:

Photocopy or hand-copy this seal on parchment or rag bond. Carry it in a little bag with cinnamon and Balm of Gilead buds. This should be your talisman to stop fear. You can also add powdered Fearlessness and Confidence incense. When you feel free of fear, burn the seal and incense, bury the bag, and send up your thanks for this gift.

∾ HAPPINESS AND JOY ∾

If being unhappy is a persistent problem, please consider getting professional help (physical and/or mental) to get you up and out of this problem. In therapy, I like to supplement verbal treatment with growth-oriented tools such as candles for quicker and deeper healing. Please also read the sections on Emotional Healing and After a Birth (referring to PMS), pages 125 and 106 respectively.

This symbol not only brings happiness, but blessings.

IDEAL TIMING:
Anytime.

SUGGESTED CANDLE AND GLITTER COLORS:
Yellow or gold for joy. Pink for sweetness and friendship.

OILS AND/OR INCENSES:
Bliss, Has No Hanna, Cherry, Bergamot, Sun, Bast, Frankincense, Vanilla, Joy and Contentment, or Thyme.

MEDITATION:
Envision having the most joyous time alone or with a special person. Summon a big dose of golden, glowing light to fill you up. Feel it turning purple as it pours into your crown chakra; see chart on page 21. Please say "please" and "thank you" to whomever you believe in and whoever spiritually helps you with your request. Always emphasize that you understand that this is merely a request—a strong request—but you know that whatever happens is for the highest good and may not manifest exactly as you envision it.

ADDITIONAL SUGGESTIONS:

Photocopy or hand-copy this seal on parchment or rag bond. Carry it in a little bag with marigold flowers, chunks of frankincense, rose petals, and powdered Bliss incense. When you feel free of woe, burn the seal and incense, bury the bag and its contents, and send up your thanks for this gift.

~ PEACE AND HARMONY ~

This symbol is good for meditation and for solving problems that need peace and harmony. Concentrating on the symbol and using it on the candle can bring an atmosphere of harmony. Reduces drama!

IDEAL TIMING:
Anytime.

SUGGESTED CANDLE AND GLITTER COLORS:
Use white or blue for peace. Harmony can be represented by green for the balance of the heart chakra.

OILS AND/OR INCENSES:
Pax/Peace/Osiris; Peace, Protection, and Blessings; Stress Reduction; or Lotus.

MEDITATION:
Envision a soft bed of white pillows. Feel yourself sinking into the bed slowly as if you are being lowered gently from the sky. Feel all the tension leaving your feet. Work up through your body, part by part, until you reach your crown. Bathe in the rich peace and calm. If there is a situation that particularly needs peace and harmonizing, envision it working out in a peaceful way. Pray for peace in your house, the neighborhood, country, and world. Please say "please" and "thank you" to whomever you believe in and whoever spiritually helps you with your request. Always emphasize that you understand that this is merely a request—a strong request—but you know that whatever happens is for the highest good and may not manifest exactly as you envision it.

ADDITIONAL SUGGESTIONS:

Take a hot bath and put in a few drops of Lotus oil. Light a white candle and envision harmony and peace. Feel it seep into your body. Also, refer to Emotional Healing on page 125.

Photocopy or hand-copy this seal on parchment or rag bond. You can carry it in a little bag. When you feel the peace and harmony, burn the seal, bury the bag, and send up your thanks for this gift.

≈ SPIRITUAL ENLIGHTENMENT
AND INNER PEACE ≈

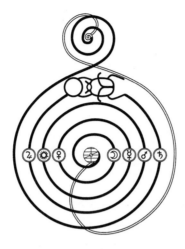

Spiritual enlightenment can come through one's meditations and dreams. If you have psychic abilities, you probably acknowledge that the gift comes from a higher divine source. If you have not allowed time for the higher source to speak through you, you are probably getting messages through your dreams. The dreams may even bring anxiety or be disturbing. This is a sign that you are not in touch with the higher realms and they are calling you. Of course, you could also be working out some issues on this plane as well. Either way, it is time to seek and be open to higher wisdom. Spending more time meditating or being otherwise in touch with your higher forces will reduce their need to get your attention at night. Please also refer to the section on incense, page 23; spirits seem to respond to it. Incense can also act as a focus for the seeker and a gift to the gods.

We are not hermits. The highest spiritual path in this day and age is to be involved on the earthly plane to save and change our wounded planet. Many people need contact with a spiritual person. See if you can fit in a good deed and spiritual act into every week. You will find as you are more and more in touch with your spirituality, you will be living spiritually. And it feels different—you're more relaxed, less hurts you, and life is more manageable. With your good deeds and love in the world, you will keep advancing and feeling more peace. Giving should be measured, however. Balance and give what you can—not what you cannot (don't use all your energy), and it shouldn't be a "should." Keep all things in balance and moderation. Revitalize yourself with exercise, a good diet, enough sleep, and some fun!

IDEAL TIMING:
Anytime.

SUGGESTED CANDLE AND GLITTER COLORS:

White, silver, purple, yellow, and gold.

OILS AND/OR INCENSES:

Mystic Seer; Lotus; High Priestess; Flying; Isis; Pax/Peace/Osiris; Egyptian Temple; Mimosa; Sun; Moon; Myrrh; Frankincense; Peace, Protection, and Blessings; Sweet Magical Trance; or Sandalwood.

MEDITATION:

During meditation, envision wisdom or inner peace coming to you in the most warm and embracing way. Feel the knowing pour into your chakras and through your cells. Before you sleep, thank your higher sources for the anticipated prophetic dreams, visions, and astral travel. There are many mental exercises you can do to improve meditation skills and hasten your ability to relax. You can envision geometric shapes, first as two-dimensional forms, then as three-dimensional. Or, envision writing the letters of the alphabet, one by one, on a blackboard. Draw a circle around each one. Carefully erase the circle and then the letter. Replace with the next letter in the alphabet. Repeat procedure. This trance will be very deep. At the end of the alphabet give yourself a positive suggestion (which you plan before your meditation). See Stress Reduction, Weight Loss, and Breaking Patterns and Addictions on page 131 for how to form affirmations. Always say "please" and "thank you" to whomever you believe in and whoever spiritually helps you with your request. Always emphasize that you understand that this is merely a request—a strong request—but you know that whatever happens is for the highest good and may not manifest exactly as you envision it.

ADDITIONAL SUGGESTIONS:

This difficult symbol (from Athanasius Kircher's *Oedipus Aegyptiacus*) is hard to draw. Don't worry about how it looks—just get into the *process* of drawing it. Start in the center and draw the spiral, clockwise. The process of drawing this will bring the trance and enlightenment. Don't forget to include your astrological name and sign.

Put mugwort leaves or drops of mimosa oil under your pillow for prophetic dreams. Burning Flying or Mystic Seer incenses will help promote visions.

Photocopy or hand-copy this seal on parchment or rag bond. Place it in a bag with mugwort leaves. Write your name on the paper. Store this bag in a drawer and carry it with you when you are seeking wisdom. Replace the mugwort in the bag with fresh leaves yearly.

~ EMOTIONAL HEALING ~

Healing takes many forms—emotional, physical, and/or spiritual—and is needed universally. The division between emotional and physical injuries is artificial. I suggest that when any healing work is needed, address both, but emphasize whichever is prominent at the moment. Obviously, if you have suffered a loss or are fighting with relatives, employees, bosses, or lovers, healing directed to your emotional self is crucial. You may need to reconcile the past in order to heal. Or, you may just need to heal and love yourself. Although these are emotional injuries, they can take a toll on your health. On the other hand, if you have been physically hurt, your body needs healing even though your mind plays a large curative role.

If you experience persistent emotional trouble, please seek verbal, art, music, or dance therapy, if only to get you through this tough time. Also, be sure that your emotional difficulties do not stem from an underlying physical condition. Please consult a health professional.

IDEAL TIMING:

Anytime.

SUGGESTED CANDLE AND GLITTER COLORS:

Yellow is for happy feelings between parties. It's also good if you have low energy levels or are depressed. White or pink is good for healing a broken heart; also see Loss, Grieving, and Acceptance on page 133.) All three colors are good for healing love relationships. Silver or white heals love sickness. Orange or copper can also be good for communication.

OILS AND/OR INCENSES:

Kindly Spirit, Sun, Joy and Contentment, Healing, Marjoram, Camellia (or for women, Camellia mixed with Venus oil), Grieving and Comfort oil, Cyclamen, Balm of Gilead, Coriander, Coping, or Anger Be Gone.

MEDITATION:

If it is a new, full, or waxing moon, meditate upon building strength and emotional health. If it is waning, send obstacles to healing away. Envision the "dis-ease" leaving the body. Send problems away from you. See warmth healing your relationships and light filling your feeling of emptiness. Please say "please" and "thank you" to whomever you believe in and whoever spiritually helps you with your request. Always emphasize that you understand that this is merely a request—a strong request—but you know that whatever happens is for the highest good and may not manifest exactly as you envision it.

ADDITIONAL SUGGESTIONS:

If you are healing relationships, you can sprinkle Anger Be Gone powder or burn Stress Reduction incense in your home. In home and work situations I also recommend wearing Kindly Spirit oil so that people will let up on you and see your good points. Please also refer to Stop Fighting and Stress on page 65. This is excellent for easing tensions. Also see A Blast of Sunlight and Energy on page 129.

Photocopy or hand-copy this seal on parchment or rag bond. You can carry it in a little bag. When you feel healthy, burn the seal, bury the bag, and send up your thanks for this gift.

❧ PHYSICAL HEALING ❧

Be sure to read the beginning of this section, about healing and asking permission of the ill person before you do a healing. This symbol not only sends physical healing, skills to the healer, and rapid recovery, but love and peace.

As explained in the Emotional Healing section, the mind and body are completely interconnected. When you are having emotional difficulties, you have to be aware of your physical health. If necessary *please consult a health professional* and improve your fitness and nutritional habits. Health can influence your entire life.

IDEAL TIMING:

Anytime.

SUGGESTED CANDLE AND GLITTER COLORS:

You can choose your candle's color by referring to the chart of chakras on page 21. In general, yellow can be used for respiratory difficulties. White is an all-around healer, especially for bones. Green for female and heart problems, blue for anger and stress-related disorders, and purple for expansion and bringing in the divine.

OILS AND/OR INCENSES:

Healing, Conquering Glory, Sun, or Lotus (especially for animals).

MEDITATION:

During a new, waxing, or full moon, meditate upon building strength and health. Envision the best medical care. See all treatments healing the site(s) of injury or disease. If you are doing this during a waning moon, send obstacles to healing away. Envision the disease leaving the person's body. Please say "please" and "thank you" to whomever you believe in and whoever spiritually helps you with your request. Always emphasize that you understand that this is merely a request—a strong request—but you know that whatever happens is for the highest good and may not manifest exactly as you envision it.

ADDITIONAL SUGGESTIONS:

You can burn Kyphi incense during the waning moon to send illness away. Carve the ill person's name and astrological sign into the candle wax. If a disease or tumor needs to be spiritually arrested or constricted in development, it would be advisable to light the candle on Saturday, the day of Saturn.

Photocopy or hand-copy this seal on parchment or rag bond. Carry it in a little bag with violets, mustard seeds, and marjoram. Put the seal in the bag with powdered Healing incense. When health has come, burn the seals and incense, scatter the violets and herbs on a body of water or the earth, thank your physicians and friends, bury the little bag, and send up your thanks for this gift.

∿ A BLAST OF SUNLIGHT AND ENERGY ∿

This symbol gives a blast of energy and light. It cleanses and revitalizes and gives new strength and verve. Carve the designated person's name and astrological sign in the seal's center.

IDEAL TIMING:
Waxing moon.

SUGGESTED CANDLE AND GLITTER COLORS:
Yellow or gold for the sun. Pink for a blast to your love life. Orange for a boost to your success.

OILS AND/OR INCENSES:
Rosemary, Carnation, Vanilla, Bountiful Prosperity, Sun, or Success Blast.

MEDITATION:
Feel your strength and energy returning. Envision energy as a yellow glow and watch it fill every inch of your body, even your fingertips and toes. Please say "please" and "thank you" to whomever you believe in and whoever spiritually helps you with your request. Always emphasize that you understand that this is merely a request—a strong request—but you know that whatever happens is for the highest good and may not manifest exactly as you envision it.

ADDITIONAL SUGGESTIONS:

Burn the candle by your bath. Pour in a small amount of Carnation or Rosemary oils. Relax and feel the light surround you.

Photocopy or hand-copy this seal on parchment or rag bond. Give an appropriate offering. Carry the seal in a little bag. When you feel the cleansing and energy of the sun, burn the seal, bury the bag, and send up your thanks for this gift.

~ STRESS REDUCTION, WEIGHT LOSS, AND BREAKING PATTERNS AND ADDICTIONS ~

This seal is for letting go of stress, weight patterns, destructive patterns, and addictions. Do this candle and envision having a joyous time—free of these problems.

Bring in a big dose of golden, glowing light and let it fill you. Feel it pouring into your crown chakra. Feel yourself being free of any urges or cravings or stress. Clear your mind and sit quietly. Practice counting back from fifty, concentrating only on the numbers. Don't let your mind wander. Anytime it does, just go back to the task. By the time you get to one, you will be thoroughly relaxed. Once you become accustomed to being relaxed, reduce the task. Count back from ten to one. You can do this silently anywhere, at any time, to get instantly relaxed and gain control over your life. Do this before you are tempted to overindulge in your "vice." Before eating, for example, silently count from ten to one. At one, while thoroughly relaxed, say to yourself some affirmation such as "I will feel full on less food." If you're going to a party where drugs or alcohol will be present, affirm to yourself, "I will have fun because of the closeness of friends," or something that fits you. If you're under pressure, you can suggest to yourself things like, "I can do my work better if I take breaks and relax" or "I feel my muscles loosening and the tension leaving my body." Be sure to exclude the word *not* from any of your affirmations. Your mind erases that word. It also hates *should*. Phrase your affirmations as positively as possible. No scolding, critical, or lecturing affirmations!

IDEAL TIMING:
Waning moon.

SUGGESTED CANDLE AND GLITTER COLORS:

Yellow for cleansing and the strength needed to fight and break addictions. Blue or green to relax. Red for mastering the situation. Purple or white for protection, letting go, and handing it over to god, goddess, or whomever you work with spiritually.

OILS AND/OR INCENSES:

Use Letting Go or Master oil for breaking addictions to food, drugs, love, etc. For reducing stress, use Stress Reduction, Clove, Chamomile, Lavender, or Pax/Peace/Osiris.

ADDITIONAL SUGGESTIONS:

Also use the symbol in Part VI, Success, for "Clarity, Focus, Decision Making, Studying, Direction, and Concentration" on page 170. Please say "please" and "thank you" to whomever you believe in and whoever spiritually helps you with your request. Always emphasize that you understand that this is merely a request—a strong request—but you know that whatever happens is for the highest good and may not manifest exactly as you envision it.

Photocopy or hand-copy this seal on parchment or rag bond. You can carry it in a little bag. When you feel free of stress, weight, patterns, or addiction, burn the seal and send up your thanks for this gift.

~ LOSS, GRIEVING, AND ACCEPTANCE ~

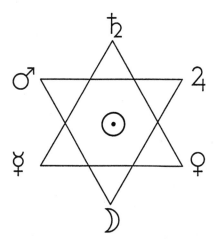

According to the Object Relations Theory in psychology, the feeling of being connected to another human being is what motivates us and gives us a reason to be. I believe that the largest task in our lives is to separate, especially from our parents. We are continually separating in different ways from different relationships throughout our lives. Yet, letting go and not connecting can be wrenching. Great growth, however, is the result of each loss and transition. When you are feeling sorrow, know that you are at sea in the pools of tears cried through the ages for all those that have been lost or died. Sorrow is not only one of the highest spiritual states, but one of the deepest sources of growth and wisdom.

This candle is for you and *your* grief process. If you want to do a candle for someone who has died, refer to the next entry, Letting Go, Transitions, and Passages.

IDEAL TIMING:
Waning moon.

SUGGESTED CANDLE AND GLITTER COLORS:
White and silver.

OILS AND/OR INCENSES:
Cyclamen, Joy and Contentment, Clove, Grieving and Comfort, Apple, Benzoin, Hyacinth, New Beginnings, Letting Go, or Balm of Gilead.

MEDITATION:
Your meditation will, of course, be very personal. If you are doing this because of a loss

in your life, you might wish the person a safe and peaceful farewell. Try to understand his or her leaving, whether it is a separation or a death. Know that a new and full life awaits you—even without them. You have to continue. There are things for you to do. And, know that you will never completely lose them; they are alive whenever you want them to be, in your memory. Please say "please" and "thank you" to whomever you believe in and whoever spiritually helps you with your request. Always emphasize that you understand that this is merely a request—a strong request—but you know that whatever happens is for the highest good and may not manifest exactly as you envision it.

ADDITIONAL SUGGESTIONS:

You can also perform a separate ritual for your lost loved one. Say what you would like to say to them if they were present. Write their name on a piece of paper and burn it. Let it go.

❧ LETTING GO, TRANSITIONS, AND PASSAGES ❧

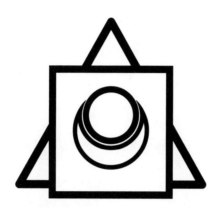

This is an excellent symbol for many times in one's life. You could be transitioning from one job, marriage, place, and mind-set to another. Your transition or passage could be the way to a whole other way of life. Yet transitions and changes are difficult, even when they are for the better.

Death is one of our transitions. Usually when someone or a relationship has died, there is a need to mark the event and make transitions as smooth as possible. When someone has died, or on the anniversary of a loved one's death (or even a breakup you can't shake), light a white candle (anointed with a suitable oil like Joy and Contentment) in the early evening, to commemorate the loss. Make your prayers for that person as formal or casual as you feel. Pray for the person and also your continued healing and growth, the result of knowing *and* losing them. If you have questions for them, ask. Speak to them and tell them how you feel and what you are thinking. Send your love and peace. Let them go.

IDEAL TIMING:
Waning moon.

SUGGESTED CANDLE AND GLITTER COLORS:
White and silver.

OILS AND/OR INCENSES:
Letting Go, New Beginnings, or Cyclamen.

MEDITATION:

Envision your (or someone else's) transition bringing you growth and happiness. Look in the mirror. See your face. Does it look sad now? Bring light to it. Try to smile. Fill your face with joy. Remember how it looks, even if you can't achieve a smile now. Please say "please" and "thank you" to whomever you believe in and whoever spiritually helps you with your request. Always emphasize that you understand that this is merely a request—a strong request—but you know that whatever happens is for the highest good and may not manifest exactly as you envision it.

ADDITIONAL SUGGESTIONS:

You can put three drops of Coping oil in the water with which you mop the floor if you're having difficulty adapting to changes in life.

Photocopy or hand-copy this seal on parchment or rag bond. Carry it in a little bag for smooth transitions and letting go of whatever is blocking you. When you have made your passage, burn the seal and send up your thanks for this gift.

～ NEW BEGINNINGS—LIFE CHANGER ～

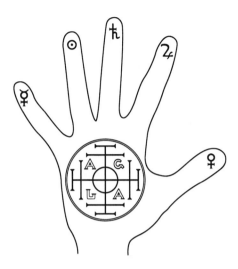

This symbol brings good luck in all the areas of your life and reverses whatever bad luck there is. It is your job to focus on each of those areas by making lists of what you would like to happen.

IDEAL TIMING:

New, waxing, and full moons.

SUGGESTED CANDLE COLORS:

Green for growth. Yellow for building a new life and joy. Purple for expansion and just rewards.

SUGGESTED GLITTER COLORS:

Thumb: Venus—green (a green thumb). Index finger: Jupiter—purple or blue. Middle finger: Saturn—black. Ring finger: Sun—yellow or gold. Little finger: Mercury—orange or copper.

OILS AND/OR INCENSES:

New Beginnings, Bountiful Prosperity, Super Fast Luck, Everything, Conquering Glory, or Blessing.

MEDITATION:

Define the new beginnings you desire. See them flooding into your life. Please say "please" and "thank you" to whomever you believe in and whoever spiritually helps you with your request. Always emphasize that you understand that this is merely a request—a strong request—but you know that whatever happens is for the highest good and may not manifest exactly as you envision.

ADDITIONAL SUGGESTIONS:

Carry or wear an ankh, the symbol of creation and new life. Find one that attracts you, whether it is found in a book, carved in wood by a friend, or purchased as jewelry from a store.

～ MOTIVATION AND WILL ～

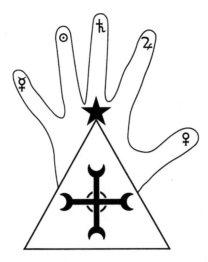

Sometimes we just need a nice swift kick. Here it is. Get prepared to finish projects and find motivation you never dreamed possible.

IDEAL TIMING:
Anytime.

SUGGESTED CANDLE AND GLITTER COLORS:
Red for the passion, drive, and motivation of Mars.

OILS AND/OR INCENSES:
Mars and Motivation, Completion, Narcissus, Master, Fearlessness and Confidence, Iris Perfume, or Sun.

MEDITATION:
On the waxing moon, envision the fulfillment of all tasks. At the waning moon, see obstacles to your achievement waning away. Write on paper why you need will and motivation. What do you want to achieve? Hold the paper and your project (if it can be held) away from you as if you were presenting it to someone. Close your eyes and envision your higher force reading your request. See the red energy of Mars travel from the paper and project, up your arms to your brain. Feel the red filling you. Now, go do it! Please say "please" and "thank you" to whomever you believe in and whoever spiritually helps you with your request. Always emphasize that you understand that this is merely a request—a strong request—but

you know that whatever happens is for the highest good and may not manifest exactly as you envision it.

ADDITIONAL SUGGESTIONS:

If your motivation and will were something red, how red would they be? Find and buy flowers that capture that color and feel proper for your candle's purpose. Place them somewhere in your home where you can see them regularly. Focus on them.

You can also photocopy or hand-copy this seal on parchment or rag bond. Carry it in a little bag with herbs sacred to Mars, such as black pepper, basil, galangal, and rosemary. When you feel your will or have achieved your goal, burn the seal, bury the bag and its contents, and send up your thanks for this gift.

~ STRENGTH ~

At times, we might simply need strength to get us through. This symbol incorporates the unity of two parts—two parts of yourself or others. Therefore, it can also be used to resolve something between two parties for the highest good.

The strength of the sun is warm, supportive, healing, and giving. The strength of Mars is powerful, forceful, and unyielding. Choose which sort of strength you need for this occasion.

IDEAL TIMING:
Waxing moon.

SUGGESTED CANDLE AND GLITTER COLORS:
Yellow for the sun. Red for Mars.

OILS AND/OR INCENSES:
Mars, Sun, Stress Reduction Seven African Powers, or Success Blast.

MEDITATION:
Bring the color of strength (yellow or red) into your body. Feel and see it filling your soul with nourishing strength and power. Please say "please" and "thank you" to whomever you believe in and whoever spiritually helps you with your request. Always emphasize that you understand that this is merely a request—a strong request—but you know that whatever happens is for the highest good and may not manifest exactly as you envision it.

ADDITIONAL SUGGESTIONS:

Surround yourself with the color yellow or red, whichever feels appropriate for your purpose. Wear it and when it's edible, eat and drink it.

You can photocopy or hand-copy this seal and carry it in a little bag. When you feel strong, burn the seal, bury the bag, and send up your thanks for this gift.

~ REBIRTH ~

This is the same symbol that is used for a literal safe birth and delivery in the section covering Pregnancy. It brings birth and rebirth to those who need a boost or renewal.

IDEAL TIMING:

Waxing or dark moon.

SUGGESTED CANDLE AND GLITTER COLORS:

White or silver for Mother Goddess and moon energy.

OILS AND/OR INCENSES:

Moon, Healing, Pax/Peace/Osiris, Clarity, New Beginnings, Rebirth and Rejuvenation, or Cyclamen.

MEDITATION:

Meditate upon what you will be when reborn. Start again as you light this candle. Thank the crone and dark goddesses for the power we have to create and be born. Please say "please" and "thank you" to whomever you believe in and whoever spiritually helps you with your request. Always emphasize that you understand that this is merely a request—a strong request—but you know that whatever happens is for the highest good and may not manifest exactly as you envision it.

ADDITIONAL SUGGESTIONS:

Perform a charitable act. Give flowers to someone. Give flowers to your candle. Plant some flowers or trees. Bring life into the world.

Photocopy or hand-copy a pinecone, frog, or this symbol to carry in a little bag. You can also carry a real pinecone. The frog may come to you in the form of a figurine or jewelry. When the rebirth happens, carry the bag and mark this day as the second time you were born. One year and a day from your second birth, burn the seal and send up your thanks for this gift.

∼ OILS FOR PERSONAL GROWTH AND HEALING ∼

Please check the Appendix, page 204, for more extensive explanations.

ANGER BE GONE helps one let go of pent-up anger, annoyances, and hostile feelings.

APPLE brings friends, peace of mind, relaxation, and successful projects.

BALM OF GILEAD helps you let go, heals a broken heart, and brings radiance. Good for soothing, relaxing, and renewing the spirit.

BAST brings the exquisite joy of little blessings.

BENZOIN brings a sense of personal power, peace of mind, and freedom from outside worries. It is also a highly spiritual scent that can send your thoughts and prayers to loved ones who have passed away.

BERGAMOT, the refined citrus scent in Earl Grey tea, brings joy, confidence, lightness, and healing.

BLESSING is calming and brings blessings into one's life.

BLISS brings exquisite bliss and joy! Great for beating the blues!

BOUNTIFUL PROSPERITY brings great plenty in all areas of life.

CAMELLIA is great for personal growth, confidence, and a heightened sense of self.

CARNATION rejuvenates, refreshes, and energizes, but also soothes, calms, and heals.

CHAMOMILE is very, very, very relaxing.

CHERRY brings joy, confidence, humor, and life. Gets rid of worries.

CLARITY helps the seeker understand the issues at hand and see them clearly.

CLOVE is good for inspiration, memory, protection, inner strength, and courage.

COMPLETION brings negotiations to a close. Good for decision and deal making.

CONQUERING GLORY overcomes whatever obstacles are in the way to your success.

COPING brings the ability to deal with the situations at hand and whatever is thrown at you.

CORIANDER heals and stimulates the mind.

CYCLAMEN is for safe passage and all kinds of transitions.

EGYPTIAN TEMPLE creates a sacred space.

EVERYTHING is for love, money, protection, clarity, wishing, and joy—you name it!

FEARLESSNESS AND CONFIDENCE conquers fears and insecurities. Pushes projects forward.

FRANKINCENSE brings the sun—prosperity, healing, and success.

GRIEVING AND COMFORT eases the pain of losing a loved one.

HAS NO HANNA eliminates depression and poverty. This oil includes in the bottle an open safety pin to catch the wealth and plenty.

HEALING attunes one to preserving health and healing the body and mind.

HIGH PRIESTESS brings forth mysteries that have not been revealed. High spirituality.

HYACINTH eases obsessions, depression, grief, and nightmares.

IRIS PERFUME increases determination, concentration, and will.

ISIS was created for the Egyptian goddess of love, rebirth, and creation.

JOY AND CONTENTMENT injects the daily jolt of joy and empowerment you need. Banishes depression.

KINDLY SPIRIT makes people like you and be sympathetic to your cause.

KYPHI is good for healing and banishing negativity.

LAVENDER relaxes and brings contentment.

LETTING GO helps you to let go gently and completely. Let go of the old; bring in the new.

LOTUS gives gifts of healing, spirituality, protection, and insights.

MARJORAM overcomes depression and strengthens love. Surrounds you in an atmosphere of loyalty and security.

MARS AND MOTIVATION gets you moving and motivated. Gives energy and fearlessness.

MASTER helps one to master a situation and gain control. Great for addictions and overeating.

MIMOSA brings out dreams and subconscious desires.

MOON is a wonderful blend for healing and worshipping the moon goddess.

MYRRH purifies space and consecrates objects.

MYSTIC SEER opens the inner doors to light and wisdom.

NARCISSUS gives confidence, strength, self-love, fearlessness, and will.

NEW BEGINNINGS brings about new starts in general or specific areas of life.

PAX/PEACE/OSIRIS creates a positive, peaceful atmosphere around the wearer.

PEACE, PROTECTION, AND BLESSINGS brings all three! A powerful shield of light.

REBIRTH AND REJUVENATION brings a new you and boosts confidence.

ROSEMARY gives a sense of strength, being loved, and well-being.

SAINT JUDE is to be used when anything you are endeavoring seems impossible.

SANDALWOOD is the all-purpose spiritual scent. Grants wisdom and creativity.

SEVEN AFRICAN POWERS empowers you in seven areas of your life.

STRESS REDUCTION reduces the stress, tension, and fighting.

SUCCESS BLAST yields a serious blast of success. It gets careers and projects moving.

SUN bathes the wearer in the joy and warmth of the sun: health, wealth, happiness, and success.

SUPER FAST LUCK reverses bad luck and brings fast luck to any endeavor.

SWEET MAGICAL TRANCE is good for visions, astral travel, and prophetic dreams.

THYME brings irresistibility, courage, and compassion.

VANILLA is good for being fabulous, strong, and lucky.

VENUS brings warmth, friendship, and a sense of being loved and secure.

◆

PART VI

SUCCESS

I n this society, production is paramount; it is often a measure of our worth. It is difficult to be accepted for who we are, separate from our title or accomplishments.

Definitions of success and the steps to reach it vary. Your choice to start a business may differ greatly from someone else's. Use "Success" to make connections, get customers, or sell your goods, or define what "success" means to you personally. You may need "Money Drawing and Debt Collection" to gather money, find investors, or get payments owed to you. Use "Finding or Selling a House, Apartment, or Business" to sell your house or "Completion of Any Project/Sign or Finalize a Contract or Deal" if you are ready to close on a house. "Good Fortune and Reversing Bad Luck" overcomes a run of bad fortune. Or you may need a series of candles addressing many aspects. Outline your game plan. Artists may start with "Creativity and Inspiration" and end up with "Performers, Recognition, Fame, and

C. F. Riggs-Bergesen

A carved candle with glitter for success.

Connections." Start with one approach and list the seals that pertain to it. Rank them as to how helpful each of them will be. Since this is a process, your game plan will change as the candle burns and you learn. Assess what is important and reassess your plan with the new information. Be clear and choose one or two symbols to start. Don't load the candle with symbols. Keep track of all your intentions and goals. Your achievements will build; go through the steps. Business transactions can use the energy of Saturn, Mercury, Venus, Sun, and/or Jupiter depending on the flavor of what is needed. You can use the color or the day of the planet to set the tone. For example, you can use Saturn (black or brown) for stability in a business transaction or closing. For fostering business communication and opportunities, use Mercury (orange).

~ SUCCESS ~

This seal can attract customers and bring success to you and your business. It can make you a success at your job and it helps with all the steps to your crowning success.

IDEAL TIMING:

Anytime, especially the new moon.

SUGGESTED CANDLE AND GLITTER COLORS:

Orange (Mercury) for smooth transactions, open doors, improved business, success, and more opportunities. Purple (Jupiter) for expansion. Green (Venus) for growth and money. Yellow (sun) for recognition, joy, and wealth. Brown for stabilizing success. Black for eliminating negativity and finalizing contracts. If you are uncomfortable with black, use orange or brown.

OILS AND/OR INCENSES:

Success, Success Blast, Sun, Arabka Soudagar, Bountiful Prosperity, Crown of Success, Super Fast Luck, Jupiter, Mercury, Wish Fulfillment, Lucky Job, Conquering Glory, Seven African Powers, Shi Shi, San Ramon, or Frankincense.

MEDITATION:

During the waxing moon, see your business flourishing and cash flow increasing. Envision customers partaking of your services and coming back. Fill yourself with the energy and strength necessary to do your part on the physical plane to conduct business. During the waning moon, send away hassles, obstacles, and poverty. Envision overcoming any obstacles to your accomplishments. Please say "please" and "thank you" to whomever you believe in and whoever spiritually helps you with your request. Always emphasize that you understand that this is merely a request—a strong request—but you know that whatever happens is for the highest good and may not manifest exactly as you envision it.

ADDITIONAL SUGGESTIONS:

Burn Shi Shi, Jupiter, Money, or Arabka Soudagar incense in your business to attract and expand business. Post this seal near your cash register or financial center. Explore the principles of feng shui to increase your prosperity.

Photocopy or hand-copy this symbol onto golden paper of any kind. When success picks up or arrives, give to a charity, burn the seal, and send up your thanks for this gift.

~ NEW OPPORTUNITIES AND OPEN DOORS ~

This symbol not only brings new opportunities, it gives the wisdom and clarity to assess the value of the opportunity.

IDEAL TIMING:

Anytime.

SUGGESTED CANDLE AND GLITTER COLORS:

Yellow for the clarity of the sun. Purple or blue for the expansiveness and wisdom of Jupiter. Green for the attraction and drawing power of Venus.

OILS AND/OR INCENSES:

Bountiful Prosperity, New Beginnings, Ylang Ylang, Success Blast, Jupiter, Super Fast Luck, Lucky Hand, or Blessing.

MEDITATION:

Please say "please" and "thank you" to whomever you believe in and whoever spiritually helps you with your request. Always emphasize that you understand that this is merely a request—a strong request—but you know that whatever happens is for the highest good and may not manifest exactly as you envision it.

ADDITIONAL SUGGESTIONS:

Photocopy or hand-copy this seal. When your opportunity comes, burn the seal and send up your thanks for this gift.

❧ GETTING A PERFECT JOB ❧

This is good for getting a new job or the desired promotion at your present job. Burn the candle while creating your résumé, sending it, or doing job-related phone work.

This symbol can awaken admiration in others. Include your name and astrological sign on the candle. If you have a specific job in mind, be sure to include it along with the phrase "or something even better." You never know; the perfect job may not have been offered yet.

IDEAL TIMING:

Anytime.

SUGGESTED CANDLE AND GLITTER COLORS:

Green, if the emphasis is pay. Orange, if you need an opportunity for a great job or someone to choose you for the position.

OILS AND/OR INCENSES:

Lucky Job, Sun, Success, Conquering Glory, Ylang Ylang, Money, Crown of Success, Super Fast Luck, Success Blast, Bountiful Prosperity, or Joy and Contentment.

MEDITATION:

At the waxing moon, build opportunities; and at the waning, send away stumbling blocks to success. Please say "please" and "thank you" to whomever you believe in and whoever spiritually helps you with your request. Always emphasize that you understand that this is merely a request—a strong request—but you know that whatever happens is for the highest good and may not manifest exactly as you envision it.

ADDITIONAL SUGGESTIONS:

Make a list of all the aspects of your ideal job. Hold that list or an advertisement for a desired job between your two palms. Close your eyes and envision what makes it perfect, and see yourself sitting in your new workplace. Once you have a job in mind, use the "Choose Me" symbol on page 156.

Photocopy or hand-copy this seal on parchment or rag bond. Carry it in a little bag with a High John the Conqueror root. This talisman is especially powerful for making a good impression at a job interview or audition and for getting the best job. When you get the job, burn the seal, bury the bag and root, and send up your thanks for this gift.

∾ CHOOSE ME ∾

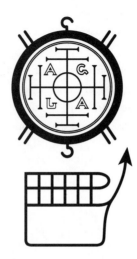

This symbol is great for being chosen for jobs and various titles. You can also use it if you want to be chosen as a tenant by building boards and landlords (home, commercial spaces, co-ops, condos, and apartment buildings). Use this to have your application, contract, or bid accepted.

IDEAL TIMING:

Anytime.

SUGGESTED CANDLE AND GLITTER COLORS:

Orange for open doors and success.

OILS AND/OR INCENSES:

Conquering Glory, Kindly Spirit, Venus, Success, Sun, or Attraction.

MEDITATION:

Pray that you are chosen for this position for the highest good of everyone involved. You don't want to be chosen over another if there is someone fated or better for the job, apartment, etc. You don't want the karma of someone losing his or her job or house, so that you can get it. Please say "please" and "thank you" to whomever you believe in and whoever spiritually helps you with your request. Always emphasize that you understand that this is merely a request—a strong request—but you know that whatever happens is for the highest good and may not manifest exactly as you envision it.

ADDITIONAL SUGGESTIONS:

Photocopy or hand-copy this seal and carry it in a little bag with a High John the Conqueror root. This is especially powerful for making a good impression. You can have it in a pocket during an interview. When you achieve your goal, burn the seal and send up your thanks for this gift.

~ MONEY DRAWING AND DEBT COLLECTION ~

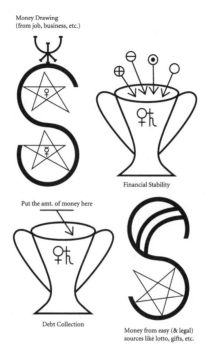

Use these symbols to draw money to you. The important part is being specific with your request. Decide upon the *minimum* amount you need. Carve that amount on to your candle and add, "or even more would be appreciated," but concentrate on your minimum. That gives the gods a format with which to work. Be sure to say "please" and "thank you" for your request. Remember, for money candles to work, it is essential to make offerings. You cannot get if you do not give. Also, continue to do your work on the earthly plane so that will be one source of the incoming cash. Don't just sit at home because you know that big Lotto payment is on its way. You can light a money candle on most days of the week: Tuesday, Mars; Wednesday, Mercury; Thursday, Jupiter; Friday, Venus; Saturday, Saturn; and Sunday, sun. The moon, Monday's celestial connection, does not deal with money and wealth, just your emotions and soul. These symbols for money will work anytime, but if you want to get really specific, consult an astrology calendar to see when Mercury is in retrograde. For around three weeks, three to four times per year, because of an optical illusion created by the orbital rotation of the earth, the planet Mercury appears to be rotating in reverse. During this time there can be blocks and miscommunications. It reverses whatever was going on—good or bad—before the retrograde. Therefore, it you have been blocked in your previous efforts to draw money, a retrograde is a perfect time to reverse that trend. Beware, because whatever you start anew in a retrograde can be ill conceived and go awry. Therefore, if you just started your efforts and need to draw money during a retrograde, change the Mercury glyph (the symbol in the center of the bottom star of the "Money Drawing" seal to Jupiter (the glyph on the pinky of the hand in the "New Beginnings—Life Changer" symbol on page 137.

IDEAL TIMING:
Anytime.

SUGGESTED CANDLE AND GLITTER COLORS:
Green (Venus) for attracting cash. Purple or blue (Jupiter) for large wealth and expansion. Brown (Earth) for financial stability.

OILS AND/OR INCENSES:
Money, Super Fast Luck, Has No Hanna, Oakmoss, Patchouli, Basil, Bergamot, Bayberry, Success Blast, or Conquering Glory (to remove obstacles). Add a drop of cinnamon oil to any blend to get things moving.

MEDITATION:
At waxing moon, build wealth; and at waning moons, send poverty away. Meditate upon the blocks to your financial security lifting. Please say "please" and "thank you" to whomever you believe in and whoever spiritually helps you with your request. Always emphasize that you understand that this is merely a request—a strong request—but you know that whatever happens is for the highest good and may not manifest exactly as you envision it.

ADDITIONAL SUGGESTIONS:
If receiving money seems blocked, carve your name, astrological sign, and how much money you need on a green candle. You can sprinkle a bit of calamus root in the corners of your kitchen to protect you from poverty.

Photocopy or hand-copy this seal on parchment or rag bond. When you get the cash for which you asked, burn the seal and send up your thanks for this gift.

～ CHANGING ANOTHER'S VIEW OF YOU ～

Again, this symbol is very useful when you would like someone to think better of you or see you in a different light. For example, if you are an assistant and would like to become an executive, perhaps your boss will be open to seeing you in that role. This does not make you better than you are; it just opens a new view of you.

If you feel someone dislikes you, wear Kindly Spirit and carve this seal on a yellow candle for joy. This is good to do if there have been misunderstandings and you want a chance to be heard and understood. Be sure to see how the misunderstandings occurred, what part you played in it, and why the other person feels that way. Use pink if the feelings are hostile and you would like to inject some sweetness. Also consider what else might help. Do you need better communication with the person or organization?

Again, this symbol is not to make you who you are not—just improve your image.

IDEAL TIMING:

Anytime.

SUGGESTED CANDLE AND GLITTER COLORS:

Yellow for joy and seeing you in a positive light. It's also good for recognition. Orange, if communication is the difficulty. Pink for bringing in friendship and sweetness.

OILS AND/OR INCENSES:

Kindly Spirit, Sun, Heliotrope, Joy and Contentment, Uncrossing, or Venus.

MEDITATION:

On a waxing moon, meditate upon building your image. Reduce personal and image problems during the waning moon. Please say "please" and "thank you" to whomever you believe in and whoever spiritually helps you with your request. Always emphasize that you understand that this is merely a request—a strong request—but you know that whatever happens is for the highest good and may not manifest exactly as you envision it.

ADDITIONAL SUGGESTIONS:

Photocopy or hand-copy this symbol on parchment or rag bond. When your image has changed, burn the seal and send up your thanks for this gift.

~ FINDING OR SELLING A HOUSE, APARTMENT, OR BUSINESS ~

Finding or selling the right home, apartment, or business usually needs a little push. You'll be surprised how smoothly the process goes when you meditate upon getting the right place or buyer. This is also good once you are negotiating. Also see the Completion of Any Project/Finalize a Contract or Deal section on page 164 . If you are trying to close on a house, do a candle for smooth negotiations for each party, another for your lawyer doing the best work for you, and another for the bank to accept your application and process the mortgage rapidly, etc. *You have to be persistent with this and do candles for each stage of the process.*

IDEAL TIMING:
Anytime.

SUGGESTED CANDLE AND GLITTER COLORS:
Orange to open the doors, assure success, and ensure good communication.

OILS AND/OR INCENSES:
Sun, Mercury, Attraction, Super Fast Luck, Success, Highest Opportunities and Open Doors, High John the Conqueror, Kindly Spirit, Conquering Glory, or Apartment Find.

MEDITATION:
At the waxing moon, bring suitable buyers or spaces. At the waning moon, send away whatever obstacles are present in your search. Please say "please" and "thank you" to whomever you believe in and whoever spiritually helps you with your request. Always emphasize that

you understand that this is merely a request—a strong request—but you know that whatever happens is for the highest good and may not manifest exactly as you envision it.

ADDITIONAL SUGGESTIONS:

Scents are very powerful. Real estate agents concur that they can lose a sale if a house smells bad. They suggest boiling a pan of water with lemon or cinnamon in it. Then pour the fresh smelling water into your disposal. Let the smell waft through the home, making it inviting. Don't overdo it. Avoid artificial sources such as things you plug into a socket, disinfectants, or heavily fragranced candles. Even people who are not aware or claim to have poor senses of smell are still affected and influenced by scents.

Photocopy or hand-copy this seal on parchment or rag bond. You can also add powdered Uncrossing, Success, and Protection incenses and carry it all in a little bag. When you have reached your goal, burn the seal and the incenses and send up your thanks for this gift. If you are leaving a home, respectfully let the little bag go with the last load of trash from the house. If you found an apartment, hang the bag from a window lock to bless your new home.

~ COMPLETION OF ANY PROJECT/ SIGN OR FINALIZE A CONTRACT OR DEAL ~

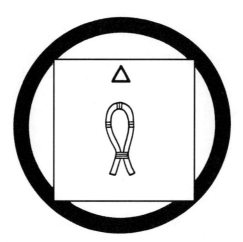

This is a symbol that incorporates many seals of completion and success. It contains the powerful Knot of Isis, as well as the synthesis of the triangle and the completion of a circle. The square within the circle signifies manifesting ideas on the earthly plane. Carve your name, astrological sign, your business's name, project name, and whatever else identifies what needs completion.

Many people believe that a contract cannot be signed when Mercury is retrograde (as explained on page 158). Sometimes this is true. But, the retrograde is not as scary or destructive as you may think. You do have to be extra careful about the small stupid details, delays, and missed appointments. On the other hand, it can bring the success you have been unable to achieve before then. The retrograde reverses whatever has been happening previously. Therefore, if business was stalled or contracts were not finalized, the retrograde will reverse that. It is not advisable to start a project during the retrograde, but if you have done your work or discovery before the retrograde, the retrograde can bring it to fruition. I suggest lighting orange candles during a retrograde in order to bring in the positive aspects of Mercury. Make friends with Mercury—don't avoid the planet.

IDEAL TIMING:
Anytime, especially Saturday.

SUGGESTED CANDLE AND GLITTER COLORS:
Orange for smooth dealings. Yellow for inspiration. Blue for relaxation.

OILS AND/OR INCENSES:

Completion; Call Me; Saturn; Mercury; Sun; Success; Peace, Protection, and Blessings; Clarity; Money; or Conquering Glory.

MEDITATION:

Envision the contract being signed, or some other kind of completion finalized for everyone's highest good. Feel the glow and relaxation of success. Please say "please" and "thank you" to whomever you believe in and whoever spiritually helps you with your request. Always emphasize that you understand that this is merely a request—a strong request—but you know that whatever happens is for the highest good and may not manifest exactly as you envision it.

ADDITIONAL SUGGESTIONS:

Try to light this on the day of Saturn (Saturday) to bring in finalization and wisdom. Carry a High John the Conqueror root to meetings about the deal and to the signing of the contract.

Photocopy or hand-copy this seal on parchment or rag bond. After you sign, burn the seal and send up your thanks for this gift.

～ CREATIVITY AND INSPIRATION ～

This symbol helps to inspire your creativity in any field or endeavor. It also can produce a strong renewal of energy. Inscribe your name and astrological sign on the candle. If a band, group, book, or creative project of some kind is involved, write its name on the candle as well.

IDEAL TIMING:

Anytime.

SUGGESTED CANDLE AND GLITTER COLORS:

Yellow for the sun and creation. Orange for Mercury, writers, overcoming blocks, and opening doors. Green for growth and purple for touching your work with the hand of divine power. Also good for expansion and new beginnings.

OILS AND/OR INCENSES:

Sweet Magical Trance, Inspiration and Creativity, Mystic Seer, Flying, Mercury, Amber, Stress Reduction, Jupiter, Sun, Fearlessness and Confidence, Mars and Motivation, Clarity, or Success Blast.

MEDITATION:

Shut off the lights and light white candles. Be quiet and sit with your work (paintings, writings, and even creatively planned business proposals). Be aware of your breathing. Spend a few minutes slowing it down and relaxing more. See if you can feel the power of your creative work. Touch your work with your left hand. (In the flow of energy, we receive through the left and put out through our right.) Let the power move in and out of you with every breath. Feel yourself becoming one with the work and the power. Please say "please" and "thank you" to whomever you believe in and whoever spiritually helps you with your request. Always emphasize that you understand that this is merely a request—a strong request—but you know that whatever happens is for the highest good and may not manifest exactly as you envision it.

ADDITIONAL SUGGESTIONS:

Also use the "Rebirth" or "A Blast of Sunlight and Energy" symbols in the Personal Growth section, pages 143 and 129, if it seems appropriate. You can wear Coping oil or sprinkle Versatile Powder around your workspace. This can inspire you to be more flexible, creative, and adaptable. This also makes you able to ride with the changes in your life and open the doors to success.

Photocopy or hand-copy this seal on a beautiful piece of parchment or rag bond. You can carry the seal in a little bag or put it in the area in which you create. When you feel free of creative blocks, burn the seal, bury the bag (or make an art piece out of it), and send up your thanks for this gift.

~ PERFORMERS, RECOGNITION, FAME, AND CONNECTIONS ~

Now that you have decided to perform, work on the basics. One must develop the skill, open the doors of opportunity, meet the right people, develop strong will and confidence, keep focused, stave off depression, maintain faith, and remain inspired to create and promote.

The business of expression is a hard business. Some of you may be happy to work in a field and be respected by your peers. Others of you may seek fame and recognition by the general public. As a gross generalization, it seems that many who are performers and strive for fame were ignored and not responded to in their youth. Many celebrities seemed not to have been heard in their early days by their role models and, even, their peers. Expression became their goal—and their fear to overcome. Your story may be different. Nonetheless, fame is recognition. Examine for yourself why recognition is a need of yours and how it can be obtained for the highest good of all involved. Fame can have a dear price.

Inscribe your name and astrological sign on the candle. If a band, group, or creative project of some kind is involved, write its name on the candle as well.

IDEAL TIMING:

Anytime, especially the waxing moon.

SUGGESTED CANDLE AND GLITTER COLORS:

Yellow for fame, success, recognition, money, and joy. Orange or copper for good skills, open doors, communications, and connections. Purple for expansion of your work.

OILS AND/OR INCENSES:

Stress Reduction, Vervain, Amber, Has No Hanna, Jupiter, Call Me, Sun, Narcissus, Wish Fulfillment, Performers and Fame, Success, Success Blast, or Fearlessness and Confidence. Some rock band members mix in a dash of Glitz, Fun, and Lust.

MEDITATION:

Rub oil on the candle, envisioning recognition and success coming from your chosen endeavor. Envision getting the job/audition/record deal/gallery/connections, etc., that will put you in the Hall of Fame—or at least keep you working! See your creativity and talent flowing easily and your being recognized and appreciated. Please say "please" and "thank you" to whomever you believe in and whoever spiritually helps you with your request. Always emphasize that you understand that this is merely a request—a strong request—but you know that whatever happens is for the highest good and may not manifest exactly as you envision it.

ADDITIONAL SUGGESTIONS:

Pour some of your favorite success oil in a bath. Take a "power bath" before an important meeting. Go out and be victorious and famous. And don't forget the little people, when your star shines! In food dishes, include a dash of herbs such as cinnamon, nutmeg, basil, or allspice.

Photocopy or hand-copy this seal on parchment or rag bond. Carry it in a little bag (to all interviews and auditions) with frankincense, myrrh, orris, and a High John the Conqueror root. Also include your name, stage name, astrological sign, and nine copper pennies (the number of completion). Place the bag in a special place between auditions or gigs. Keep this as your lucky bag for the life of your career. Over time, add things to the bag that represent good fortune. If you ever move on or retire, bury the bag, burn the seal, and send up your thanks for the experiences you had in the business.

~ CLARITY, FOCUS, DECISION MAKING, STUDYING, DIRECTION, AND CONCENTRATION ~

Carve your name and sign in the pupil of the Eye of Horus in this seal. Using this will help bring you clear and wise judgment. You can also use this seal for studying, test taking, and concentration. It helps in finding focus and direction. You might also want to carve an uncrossing candle to further rid yourself of cloudiness from external sources.

IDEAL TIMING:
Anytime.

SUGGESTED CANDLE AND GLITTER COLORS:
Yellow for the clarity and mental activity of the sun and for uncovering what is hidden. White for emotional issues. Blue for calm. Orange for openness.

OILS AND/OR INCENSES:
Clarity, Honeysuckle, Mercury, Wintergreen, Wisteria, Verbena, Iris Perfume oil, or Saint Jude.

MEDITATION:
At the waxing moon, build concentration, focus, and decision-making abilities. At the waning moon, send obstacles to decision making, concentration, and studying away. Please say "please" and "thank you" to whomever you believe in and whoever spiritually helps you

with your request. Always emphasize that you understand that this is merely a request—a strong request—but you know that whatever happens is for the highest good and may not manifest exactly as you envision it.

ADDITIONAL SUGGESTIONS:

Take a bath with salt in it before studying or making weighty decisions. If you feel it is impossible to gain clarity and you have tried as hard as you can and it *still* seems impossible, burn a Saint Jude candle along with this Clarity candle. You can make your own Saint Jude candle by using a green candle and carving into the wax, "Thank you Saint Jude for helping me with this task that seems impossible." Grocery and spiritual stores throughout the country also sell a pillar candle with a picture of Saint Jude printed on the glass.

Photocopy or hand-copy this seal on parchment or rag bond. Carry the seal and a piece of clear quartz in a bag until your decision is made or the test is taken. You can also wear yellow to bring the energy, and to remind you of the clarity. Eat a balanced diet and drink pure water, too. When you have gained the clarity you need, burn the seal, gently place the quartz and bag into a body of water, and send up your thanks for this gift.

~ GOOD FORTUNE AND REVERSING BAD LUCK ~

This seal changes the bad luck in all the areas of your life to good. Your meditation is very important to the success of this candle. Make lists. Do whatever works to mentally catalog all the areas of your life in which you need improvement. Don't worry about the bad luck; pray and meditate on good luck filling your life. It is easy to concentrate on the bad luck when things are not going your way. See if you can see the good luck you have, as well. If you really feel blocked and good fortune does not pour in, I strongly suggest doing a "Clearing, Uncrossing, and Letting Go" candle on page 183.

IDEAL TIMING:
Anytime.

SUGGESTED CANDLE AND GLITTER COLORS:
Green for money. Orange for opportunities and getting jobs. Pink for luck in love. Yellow or gold for happiness. White or silver for everything.

OILS AND/OR INCENSES:
Super Fast Luck, High John the Conqueror, Jupiter, or Lucky Lodestone.

MEDITATION:
At the waxing moon, bring luck to all areas of your life that need a good blessing. At the waning moon, send away obstacles to luck. Please say "please" and "thank you" to whomever

you believe in and whoever spiritually helps you with your request. Always emphasize that you understand that this is merely a request—a strong request—but you know that whatever happens is for the highest good and may not manifest exactly as you envision it.

ADDITIONAL SUGGESTIONS:

Photocopy or hand-copy this seal on parchment or rag bond. Carry it in a little bag. You can also include Uncrossing incense, a turquoise stone, or orange peels in the bag. When you feel free of bad luck, burn the seal, orange peels, and Uncrossing incense. What doesn't burn, throw out as a symbol of letting go of your fear. Keep the stone and the bag in a special place as a symbol of your perpetual good fortune. Burn a thank-you candle after this burns out.

~ WIN IN COURT ~

An important aspect in court is to assess your role and what you have contributed to this coming to trial. Some people say they want "justice." Justice does not necessarily mean a ruling in your favor; it means, ideally, an objective assessment of the facts. If you are not completely innocent or have made some contribution to the difficulties, be careful; justice will be served on you as well as the other party. There are things you can do whether you are guilty or not, but be honest with yourself before you employ magic, to avoid any negative consequences.

There is a great spell to do with a lemon, which can encourage a judge to rule against the other side. Cut a lemon in half, across the center. Slice a cross deep into and across the surface of one half of the lemon. Don't cut it all the way through. Write the name of the person who is against you in the court case on a thin piece of parchment about the size of a fortune cookie paper. On another such piece of parchment, write the name of the judge or court. Tear one of the pieces a little so you can fit the other piece into it and form a cross. Fit these two pieces of paper into the slices in the lemon, so they are crossing each other. Put this lemon half in a jar. Pour in vinegar, coffee grounds, and salt. Seal it with wax, if possible. Wrap it in black cloth and put in the back of a cabinet until the case is settled in your favor. Aloud, say that your desire is the judge should rule against this person filing the case against you. Thank whoever helps you spiritually and be sure to explain that you will yield to what is the highest good and whatever is your higher force's wisdom and judgment. No matter what happens, good will arise, even from an outcome you don't want. Be true and have faith.

IDEAL TIMING:

Anytime.

SUGGESTED CANDLE AND GLITTER COLORS:

If guilty, blue for mercy. If you want luck in finances, purple. If you need a judge's favor, yellow. If you need to conquer in court, brown.

OILS AND/OR INCENSES:

Success; Success Blast; Jupiter; High John the Conqueror; Peace, Protection, and Blessings; Strong Protection; Kindly Spirit; Saint Jude (if it feels impossible); Fearlessness and Confidence; Seven African Powers; Conquering Glory; Sun; or Myrrh (only if you are totally innocent; it brings justice to all).

MEDITATION:

Visualize your goal as strongly as you can, and with all your faith. Pray for it daily and put this energy into the candle. Please say "please" and "thank you" to whomever you believe in and whoever spiritually helps you with your request. Always emphasize that you understand that this is merely a request—a strong request—but you know that whatever happens is for the highest good and may not manifest exactly as you envision it.

ADDITIONAL SUGGESTIONS:

If you are guilty, pray for the fairest treatment possible. Of course, you want to get off the hook. If karma won't let you, pray for the very kindest hook. Also burn Success or Jupiter incenses the night before court. Try to keep the candle burning by leaving it with a friend to watch while you are talking to lawyers and in court.

Photocopy or hand-copy this seal on parchment or rag bond. Carry it (especially to court) in a purple cloth or bag, with a High John the Conqueror or galangal root. Keep the bag until the case is resolved. Pass on this lucky bag to a friend if you are successful, and bury the two roots. If your case didn't proceed in all the ways you would like, bury the bag and the roots together, burn the seal, and send up your thanks for whatever the judgment turns out to be.

∾ OILS FOR SUCCESS ∾

Please check the Appendix, page 204, for more extensive explanations.

AMBER brings fame, recognition, success, acclaim, happiness, protection, and money, and overcomes obstacles.

APARTMENT FIND brings the right apartment to you. A very popular city blend.

ARABKA SOUDAGAR changes bad business luck to good. Great for money drawing.

ATTRACTION can attract and find anything—job, love, friends, money, luck, apartment, etc.

BASIL draws money, cleanses, and blesses the home.

BAYBERRY is used to bring prosperity, wealth, blessings, and plenty.

BERGAMOT protects, attracts riches, and leads to new opportunities.

BLESSING (also called Altar or Trinity) is excellent for blessing objects and bringing blessings.

BOUNTIFUL PROSPERITY brings great plenty in all areas of life.

CALAMUS heals, protects, strengthens spells, and protects against poverty.

CALL ME does just what it says! It gets someone to call for business or pleasure.

CINNAMON attracts wealth, prosperity, and success. Don't wear on your skin; it's very irritating.

CLARITY increases focus, mental agility, and concentration. Great for making decisions.

COMPLETION finalizes whatever is outstanding. Good for decision and deal making.

CONQUERING GLORY overcomes all obstacles that are in the way of immediate success.

CROWN OF SUCCESS overcomes whatever is in the way of achieving your highest success.

FEARLESSNESS AND CONFIDENCE is the perfect oil for conquering fears and insecurities.

FLYING is good for free-form meditations, astral travel, and merging with the ethers.

FRANKINCENSE brings wealth, health, confidence, fearlessness, success, acclaim, and clarity.

GALANGAL is good for luck in court. Overcomes obstacles and draws money.

GLITZ, FUN, AND LUST is great for bringing seduction into your success. Use ethically and with groups of people, not one on one, because of potential manipulative aspects this may bring.

HAS NO HANNA eliminates depression and poverty. This oil includes in the bottle an open safety pin to catch the jobs and sources of money.

HELIOTROPE is for sun energy. Can both uncover and cover.

HIGHEST OPPORTUNITIES AND OPEN DOORS does just that! Great success blend.

HIGH JOHN THE CONQUEROR is for conquering, overcoming obstacles, and success.

HONEYSUCKLE can be used for a final exam. It brings eloquence and heightens the memory.

INSPIRATION AND CREATIVITY brings creation and removes blocks in the way.

IRIS PERFUME increases determination, concentration, and will.

JOY AND CONTENTMENT injects a daily jolt of empowerment. Banishes depression.

JUPITER inspires justice, fairness, mercy, expansion, vision, and truth. Can be used for winning court cases and gaining a judge's mercy.

KINDLY SPIRIT makes people like you and be sympathetic to your cause. Good for court cases.

LUCKY HAND brings luck. Be careful of what you pray for! You could get it.

LUCKY JOB finds the perfect job for you! Meditate upon what the perfect job entails. Make lists and carry a High John the Conqueror root to the interview. Good luck!

LUCKY LODESTONE attracts luck to a project and changes bad luck to good.

MARS AND MOTIVATION gets you moving and motivated, and eliminates procrastination.

MERCURY enhances communication. Opens the doors to connections, opportunities, and smooth dealings.

MINT is good for attracting money.

MONEY is used to bring money from all possible sources.

MYRRH purifies space and consecrates objects.

MYSTIC SEER brings wisdom to your business pursuits.

NARCISSUS gives confidence, strength, fearlessness and will. Great for the shy.

NEW BEGINNINGS brings about new life and starts in either all or specific areas.

NUTMEG enhances concentration, mind power, and studying.

OAKMOSS attracts money to you.

PATCHOULI is used for earthly matters and balancing. Attracts cash.

PERFORMERS brings success, fame, skill, confidence, recognition, money, and connections.

PROTECTION is an oil specifically for protection and security.

PEACE, PROTECTION, AND BLESSINGS brings all three. Be sure to be focused and clear when using it.

SAINT JUDE is good for when anything you are endeavoring seems impossible.

SAN RAMON attracts customers to your business.

SATURN is used to finalize negotiations in business or finances. Brings wisdom and strength.

SEVEN AFRICAN POWERS empowers individuals in seven personal areas of their lives. The areas should cover your main concerns such as luck in money, drawing customers and good working relationships.

SHI SHI attracts money fast. Eliminates poverty and draws cash.

STRESS REDUCTION reduces stress, tension, and fighting.

STRONG PROTECTION puts up a spiritual wall against harm. Very powerful.

SUCCESS brings success! Great for propelling business ventures and building careers.

SUCCESS BLAST yields a serious blast of success. It gets careers and projects moving.

SUN bathes the wearer in the joy and warmth of the sun. Brings health, wealth, happiness, fame, and success.

SUPER FAST LUCK reverses bad luck and brings fast luck to any endeavor.

SWEET MAGICAL TRANCE is so calming; it can feel like a sweet trance. Good for visions and magic.

UNCROSSING unhexes and eliminates all negativity and bad vibrations.

VENUS draws beauty and attraction of Venus. It also sweetens up relationships.

VERBENA is healing and cleansing. Good purification bath. Speeds mental and psychic abilities.

VERVAIN protects you and your home. Attracts wealth, success, and good dreams. Good for creativity.

WINTERGREEN brings healing, good fortune, and success in exams.

WISH FULFILLMENT grants power, favors, and that special wish. Be careful what you wish for; you could get it. It is advisable to try a more specific blend first.

WISTERIA can help you pass a test or some mental challenge with ease. It also brings blessings.

YLANG YLANG is for luck, finding good employment, and making decisions.

◆

PART VII

CLEARING, PROTECTION, AND JUSTICE

Clearing is the process of unhexing, uncrossing (removing something that crosses you), cleansing, and purifying all negativity—even curses. It clears bad karma and evil eyes. Even if bad *thoughts* are thrown at you, sometimes it can block your progress. People have described to me feeling as if they try and try and it does not seem to matter. They need a spring (or any season) cleaning. Clearings and Uncrossings work because you are working on the same level from which the curse or negativity emanates. You may not need more than one uncrossing candle and seven days of baths to change bad luck. Unbelievable, but believe it!

Uncrossing goes hand in hand with protection. You have to cleanse all negativity and protect yourself from it. Most of us experience daily bad vibes—everything from a clerk's bad mood to a jealous coworker. Maybe it is in your home. Perhaps you just feel a general sense of darkness around you. *It is not necessary to know the source of the negativity,* whether it is a literal curse (which doesn't often happen because it takes sustained energy to perform it) or merely mean thoughts. It is preferable if you do not dwell on its source at all.

Reversing the bad wishes and events will not end your misery. If you get involved in "reversing" the bad things to the person sending them, you are thinking about what those bad things are. By thinking of them, you are wishing those things to happen to the sender. Your energy is now more deeply linked to them. This can only serve to tie your energy into an endless loop. Not only have you performed dark magic, it will come back to you three times, and now they are even more intensely part of your life. Over and over. The point is to end the negativity, not continue it. So stop it. Do an uncrossing and forget about them.

If someone is wishing you ill, put up a beautiful fiery wall of protection, through which nothing can enter. (See the 1960 version of the movie *Village of the Damned* for one example of envisioning a protective mental wall.) Know that the person or people don't exist for you. Feel it. Even if you cannot feel that right away, see their workings as a joke and ineffectual drivel. They might even try to hit you one more time after you free yourself. Just know that it is one last desperate attempt to get your attention. Don't let it faze you. They've lost and they know it. The best thing is to be protected in the first place so this stupidity doesn't even enter your life. It is advisable to regularly perform protection and uncrossing candles.

Take into account that sometimes bad luck has to happen. For you to really absorb the impact of the good, the bad must happen first. From Sophocles to Alan Watts, philosophers have repeated this philosophy. It is the idea that there is always a balance and one cannot know one side of the balance without experiencing the other. Rest assured, you will be stronger after a run of bad luck than those who seemingly have it all easily handed to them. Sometimes we wonder if it has to be all bad luck. Open your eyes and appreciate the good luck around you. Really, we all do have blessings. We just have to look.

A glittered candle using the seal for Protection.

∿ CLEARING, UNCROSSING, AND LETTING GO ∿

Please read the introduction on page 181 before proceeding.

Uncrossings work. They may be all you need *even if nothing has been able to help before.* This will get rid of curses and negativity from external sources. It will also banish negativity you feel within yourself. This seal is excellent for clearing and helps you to let go of all negativity and blocks from whatever source. Carve the names and astrological signs of the people who are to receive the benefits of these candles; do not include those who are causing any problems.

IDEAL TIMING:

Waning moon.

SUGGESTED CANDLE AND GLITTER COLORS:

White is good for all clearing work, especially when you're being crossed from an external source. Black is especially good if the problem is *your own* negativity. If using black, focus all your negativity into the candle. After it burns, throw it as far away from your home as possible. Or use a color that pertains to the area in your life being crossed or affected by the negativity (green for money, pink for love, orange for success blockage, etc.).

OILS AND/OR INCENSES:

Uncrossing; Dragon's Blood; Hyssop; Camphor; Fiery Wall of Protection; Rosemary; Bay; Letting Go; Rose Geranium; Peace, Protection, and Blessing; Banishing; Purification and Rejuvenation; or Lucky Seven Root. For overcoming obstacles, use Conquering Glory, Crown of Success, or Saint Jude.

MEDITATION:

Let the negativity flow off of you. Let any blackness travel down the drain. Envision it being welcomed by Mother Earth—and cleansed in light. Concentrate upon removing all negativity and sending away whatever is crossing you, with peace. Please say "please" and "thank you" to whomever you believe in and whoever spiritually helps you with your request. Always emphasize that you understand that this is merely a request—a strong request—but you know that whatever happens is for the highest good and may not manifest exactly as you envision it.

ADDITIONAL SUGGESTIONS:

Take salt baths with camphor, white petals, and Uncrossing oil for seven nights in a row. Burn Kyphi incense for healing and banishing negativity. This combination with your candle is unbeatable. After uncrossing, it is very important to protect yourself as well. Once a month or as often as you like, take a bath in sea salt in order to maintain protection and cleansing.

Photocopy or hand-copy the seal on parchment or rag bond. You can carry it in a cloth or little bag to stop the interference, problems, and negativity. You can also add powdered Uncrossing and Protection incenses. When you feel free of negativity and/or the curse, burn the seal and incenses, bury the bag, and send up your thanks for this gift.

~ PROTECTION ~

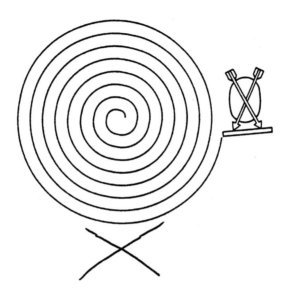

Protection, as discussed earlier in this section, is usually essential to the uncrossing process. It is certainly essential once you have been uncrossed. It is a good habit to protect yourself in a daily ritual. Use protection candles when you feel that some harm could come to you, your loved ones, pets, or possessions. Also, see the section on Safe Journeys, page 191. Please take reasonable steps to consult appropriate professionals (police, etc.) and carry protection (a loud whistle, pepper spray, and a cellular phone in your car, for example) if necessary. If you want to investigate magical protection methods further, Cunningham and Harrington's *The Magical Household* is a wonderful book. If you feel someone is sending you some negativity, magically or otherwise, light protection candles with a mirror behind them to send back any harm. Do not, however, actively get into thinking negative thoughts or sending back evil or malefic wishes. Remember that everything you do comes back to you three times. Read the Clearing, Uncrossing, and Letting Go and If You Are Tempted to Be Revengeful sections on pages 183 and 187 respectively.

IDEAL TIMING:

Anytime, but especially waxing moon to build strength.

SUGGESTED CANDLE AND GLITTER COLORS:

White for all levels of protection. Blue for peace and protection. Red for protection with the fire of Mars.

OILS AND/OR INCENSES:

Strong Protection; Tonka; Lotus; Heather (against violent and often female-oriented crimes such as rape); Thyme; Lucky Seven Root; Peace, Protection, and Blessing; or Vetivert (also a strong uncrosser).

MEDITATION:

Envision a bubble of white light around yourself, loved ones, pets, and possessions. As an example, imagine a thief trying to get into your car. See a bubble around the car and the thief being catapulted back from it as if he or she had connected with raw electricity. See the thief running away. To protect your home, envision a guardian at your door as, perhaps, a large angel with a sword. Please say "please" and "thank you" to whomever you believe in and whoever spiritually helps you with your request. Always emphasize that you understand that this is merely a request—a strong request—but you know that whatever happens is for the highest good and may not manifest exactly as you envision it.

ADDITIONAL SUGGESTIONS:

Cleanse and protect you and your space at least weekly. There are hundreds of different ways to do this. One of the most common ways is to walk counterclockwise around your dwelling, "smudging" the negativity out of your house. Counterclockwise spirals take energy out. Then, walk clockwise around your house with a blessing and protection incense to bring in blessings.

Photocopy or hand-copy the seal on parchment or rag bond. Place it in a bag with a chunk of Dragon's Blood or powdered Peace, Protection, and Blessings incense. You can hang the bag in a window or put it in your car or office—wherever it is needed. Wear a necklace of the Udjat or Eye of Horus. Replace the herbs and incense when you feel the protection is needed again. This takes different amounts of time but renew the bag's contents once a year at the minimum.

≈ IF YOU ARE TEMPTED
TO BE REVENGEFUL ≈

As Clarence Darrow, the famous lawyer and author said, "There is no such thing as justice."

You want revenge? Don't do it. Sometimes we all feel that desire for vengeance wash over us, especially in the case of heinous crime. Living a truly spiritual, ethical, magical life is choosing not to seek revenge, but to choose a far more difficult path. It is more difficult to wish the enemy blessings or to send them healing. At this point, you must call upon your higher self to find the way to let the laws of karma bring justice and let go. Since we are rarely pure of heart and without malice in these situations, do a "Clearing, Uncrossing, and Letting Go" candle with Uncrossing oil; see page 183. Read the Protection section as well, page 185. Put an end to the cycle of hatred instead of continuing it. In addition, sometimes we are not totally innocent. Assess your role in this wrongdoing. If you call down the laws of karma, will some of the justice come back to you? Don't kid yourself. Be careful. Best to cool out before you do anything. So, put yourself in the freezer. Carve your name on a white candle, drown it in honey, and put the candle in a pan of water. Then you can think clearly. Reread the Ethics section on page 9. Even without your help, the laws of karma will always bring down revenge upon a wrongdoer in a more intense way than you could even imagine. Really. You may not even know about it. So have faith and do not (do not, do not) involve yourself in wishing this person harm. Part of your (or the victim's) healing is letting go of vengeance. Then your life will move forward. Otherwise, it will not.

The following is what you can do in the process of letting go and letting the laws of karma do the dirty work, *without* your being involved or thinking about punishments and what someone "deserves" (according to your judgment). Remember, whatever you do returns to you threefold.

IDEAL TIMING:

Waning moon.

SUGGESTED CANDLE AND GLITTER COLORS:

White and silver.

OILS AND/OR INCENSES:

Letting Go, High John the Conqueror, or Myrrh.

MEDITATION:

Ask for guidance and strength to do the right thing. Have faith and hand this to a higher force. Please say "please" and "thank you" to whomever you believe in and whoever spiritually helps you with your request. Always emphasize that you understand that this is merely a request—a strong request—but you know that whatever happens is for the highest good and may not manifest exactly as you envision it.

ADDITIONAL SUGGESTIONS:

Concentrate upon moving past this. If the person is still hurting you, remove yourself physically from the situation and light protection candles. If there are psychological reasons you cannot leave, review the seals in Part III, Love, for ways to break psychological bondage. Say aloud, "It is my request that the laws of karma address this situation. I present myself as free of vengeance as I can. Please help me to heal. Please help ____ (the other person's name) to heal and to grow so that this wrong can be righted. Please wash the hatred and anger out of me so that I may continue my life. I let them go. They do not exist in my world anymore. They cannot get through my wall and I do not know they are there." Use your own phrasing. The result of thinking this way is that they will become less and less important to you. You have to move on.

~ HOUSE BLESSING AND GHOST BANISHING ~

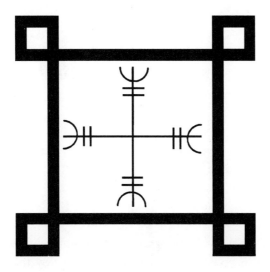

This is a must for you or as a gift to a friend with a new home. House blessings can get rid of past "bad vibes" and ghosts. It creates a new start. It cleans the space, whether it's old or new, and creates a sacred space. When you move into a new place or want to cleanse your present home, this is the perfect ritual. I suggest "smudging" by walking with a burning sage smudge stick or leaves counterclockwise around your home to banish any negativity. While you are walking, say aloud a formal or informal prayer for blessing. You will then have a clean slate. At this point, you have to bring in positive energy. Burn an incense, such as Frankincense or House Blessing to assure happiness and blessings come to your home. To renew the blessings at winter, carefully burn pine needles to cleanse and purify the home.

Many people who share their space with a ghost don't mind. It's actually cruel to the ghost. If it is your spirit guide, it's a different story; the guide is here to help you. On the other hand, a *ghost* is trapped—half here and half in the spirit realm. It is bound for some reason to a place. You have to free it, even if it is a nice companion. (Since they drain the energy of the living, you will notice their absence.) If you have a ghost, walk counterclockwise around your space burning banishing incense. Inform the ghost that he or she is not welcome and is now free to move on to a higher and better place. Repeatedly tell the ghost things like, "You are now free to go. It is time to go. Go in peace." Wish it well as you bid it farewell. Never wish the spirit harm, even if it was harming you. If it was harming you, be *very* firm, use the strongest forms of protection, and send it away with peace. Repeat this procedure daily for at least one week. Put bowls of water in every room of the house to collect the spirit as it leaves. Replenish and empty these bowls daily. Flush the water down the toilet. When preparing your candle, carve the address of the house and the names and signs of everyone in the house, including pets, into the wax.

IDEAL TIMING:

Waning moon.

SUGGESTED CANDLE AND GLITTER COLORS:

White, silver, blue, yellow, and gold.

OILS AND/OR INCENSES:

For *cleansing:* Banishing; Uncrossing; Vetivert; Peace, Protection, and Blessings; Protection; Dragon's Blood; Copal; or House Blessing.

For *blessing:* Frankincense, Sun, or House Blessing.

MEDITATION:

Spend time in your home with the lights off and no sound. Breathe in the calm. Let the feeling that you breathe in become even calmer inside you. By this process, you can transform and dissipate any tension within you or your home. If this feels difficult, try to regulate your breathing to a slower pace. When you exhale, breathe out peace into your home.

Please say "please" and "thank you" to whomever you believe in and whoever spiritually helps you with your request. Always emphasize that you understand that this is merely a request—a strong request—but you know that whatever happens is for the highest good and may not manifest exactly as you envision it.

ADDITIONAL SUGGESTIONS:

Fill small cloth bags with peppermint and rue leaves, three small chunks of frankincense, and three chunks of myrrh. Put the names of all the house's inhabitants and the phase "Please keep us sane" on the bags. Hang these over all the doors and windows of the house.

∾ SAFE JOURNEYS ∾

A suggestion, which can only help, is to bless the entire staff of the airplane when fly-ing. Pray for the pilot's clarity and wisdom, especially during takeoff and landing. Visualize a beautiful iridescent bubble of light completely surrounding the plane. This does not hinder the journey through the air; it only protects it from any harm. See it land gently and safely. This also will make you feel much more relaxed during your trip. You can do the same thing on any form of transportation. Do the same procedure when traveling in a car so others do not hit you and you arrive safely. Also, bless your car before you leave it by praying for its safekeeping. You can envision a protective bubble or, subtly of course, trace a cross, a penta-gram of protection, or a symbol of your choice as you lock the door. Envision flaming pen-tagrams on all sides of the car and by each lock. See invaders being repelled by the light.

IDEAL TIMING:
Anytime.

SUGGESTED CANDLE AND GLITTER COLORS:
White for everything. Orange or copper for the swift and smooth journey of Mercury.

OILS AND/OR INCENSES:
To enlist the help of Mercury, the mythological winged messenger, use Mercury oil. You can also use Strong Protection or Peace, Protection, and Blessings.

MEDITATION:
Please say "please" and "thank you" to whomever you believe in and whoever spiritually helps you with your request. Always emphasize that you understand that this is merely a

request—a strong request—but you know that whatever happens is for the highest good and may not manifest exactly as you envision it.

ADDITIONAL SUGGESTIONS:

Put mugwort in your luggage to protect it and yourself during a journey. Comfrey, worn or carried, also yields protection during a journey. Carry an image of Anubis and ask him to safeguard you. You can also do a devotional to the moon on the Monday before you leave on your trip. Do a thank-you candle when you return.

Photocopy or hand-copy the seal on parchment or rag bond. Carry it in a little bag with mugwort, comfrey, and powdered Protection incense. You might want to leave out the herbs and incense when you travel on planes, because of potential difficulties through security and customs. When you have arrived safely and completed your journey, burn the seal and incense, bury the bag and herbs, and send up your thanks for this gift.

～ FIND LOST OR STOLEN ITEMS OR PETS ～

Inscribe the candle with your name, astrological sign, and this seal. Also write down what possession you need returned. Anoint the candle with Conquering Glory. It is important to keep burning the candle even after the lost item or pet is returned. The candle can bring further blessings.

Also take a red cord and put thirteen knots in it. As you make each knot say, "_____ (lost object) return to me." Wear the knotted cord as a bracelet until you get your possession back.

Don't use this if you feel you simply misplaced something that you will probably find shortly.

IDEAL TIMING:
Anytime.

SUGGESTED CANDLE AND GLITTER COLORS:
Red, yellow, and orange.

OILS AND/OR INCENSES:
Magnolia, Conquering Glory, Sun, Attraction, or Mars and Motivation.

MEDITATION:
Pray to whoever helps you spiritually for assistance in returning your lost objects or pets. Please say "please" and "thank you" to whomever you believe in and whoever spiritually helps you with your request. Always emphasize that you understand that this is merely a request—

a strong request—but you know that whatever happens is for the highest good and may not manifest exactly as you envision.

ADDITIONAL SUGGESTIONS:

Carve a thank-you candle no matter what happens. Send up thanks for the things you have.

Photocopy or hand-copy this seal on parchment or rag bond and carry it in a bag. When you have found your possession, burn the seal, bury the bag, and send up your thanks for this gift.

~ OILS FOR CLEARING, PROTECTION, AND JUSTICE ~

Please check the Appendix, page 204, for more extensive explanations.

ATTRACTION attracts anything from apartments and love to lost objects and money.

BANISHING removes all negativity, bad influences, spirits, and even lingering roommates.

BAY uncrosses, removes negativity, and protects.

CAMPHOR is great for uncrossing and purification. It also brings purity and celibacy.

CLARITY increases focus, mental agility, and concentration. Great for making decisions about anything.

CONQUERING GLORY overcomes whatever obstacles are in your way. Conquer with glory.

COPAL cleanses, protects, and makes your space sacred.

CROWN OF SUCCESS overcomes whatever is in the way of achieving your highest success.

DRAGON'S BLOOD is a strong protector.

FIERY WALL OF PROTECTION sets up a wall of fire to block any attacks.

FRANKINCENSE brings wealth, health, and fearlessness. Removes mental blocks. Good for exorcism, consecration, and protection.

HEATHER is protective, especially to women.

HIGH JOHN THE CONQUEROR overcomes obstacles and brings victory, wealth, success, and acclaim.

HOUSE BLESSING is for blessing and cleansing a new home or spiritually clearing an old one.

HYSSOP protects, cleanses, and uncrosses. Can also reduce sadness and guilt.

LETTING GO helps you to let go gently and completely. Also uncrosses.

LOTUS clears, uncrosses, purifies, heals, and protects.

LUCKY SEVEN ROOT protects against being hexed by unknown enemies.

MAGNOLIA helps you to find lost possessions. Protects against psychic attacks.

MARS AND MOTIVATION gives energy, strength, and fearlessness. Protects with passion.

MERCURY opens doors to connections, opportunities, and smooth dealings.

MYRRH purifies space and consecrates objects. Brings justice.

PROTECTION protects and brings security.

PEACE, PROTECTION, AND BLESSINGS brings tranquillity, peace, protection, and blessings.

PURIFICATION AND REJUVENATION cleanses bad memories and brings fresh, positive energy.

ROSE GERANIUM is a powerful uncrossing and protecting agent. Brings blessings and courage.

ROSEMARY gets rid of bad vibes, illness, nightmares, headaches, and supposedly old age.

SAINT JUDE is to be used when anything you are endeavoring seems impossible.

STRONG PROTECTION is for the strongest protection. Use only in dire circumstances.

SUN brings health, wealth, happiness, fame, and success. Uncovers what is hidden.

THYME protects from others' negative thoughts and actions. For purification and health.

TONKA reverses bad feelings. Turns enemies into friends. Surrounds one with positive feelings.

UNCROSSING unhexes and eliminates all negativity and bad vibrations.

VETIVERT grounds and unhexes. Brings balance, tolerance, and protection from all harm.

PART VIII

◆

SAVE OUR PLANET AND GRATITUDE

C. F. Riggs-Bergesen

A carved and glittered candle for Thanks.

The following two seals are very important.

PEACE ON EARTH AND SAVE OUR PLANET

It is essential for you to send your strength and blessings to our earth for its healing. Our planet needs your help. Even if you do not see the results, know that your goodwill and efforts count.

THANKS

Giving thanks is the most neglected area of Candle Therapy and psychology. Once a crisis has abated, it is easy to forget to say thank you. Even if you think you have nothing for which to be grateful, you do. Blessings surround us. Sometimes it requires us to stop and look. They can be as important as our home and health and at other times as little as the beautiful colors in a bird's feather. Seeing the gifts will make you feel joy.

～ PEACE ON EARTH
AND SAVE OUR PLANET ～

This is a candle one can do regularly or when moved. I hope you can perform some sort of ritual at least yearly to help our Earth. This is a ritual for rebirth, protection, and continuance. It is also a seal for harmony among people. We don't have to be one homogeneous mass, but we have to get along. Pray for acceptance and tolerance of our differences. Pray about the overpopulation of our world. Pray for the people and animals that are suffering. Pray for a peaceful resolution to war and disputes between countries. Pray for what is personal to you. The way you see saving the world is important. Pray for how you can change and save the world, too.

There is incredible power in these kinds of spells. After the covens throughout England united, Hitler scrapped his plan to invade England. Certainly, the prayers of many other religious orientations were influential and answered at that time as well.

IDEAL TIMING:

Anytime. It would be wonderful if you could make this candle monthly. Each time, choose a different issue to help the earth.

SUGGESTED CANDLE AND GLITTER COLORS:

White for all aspects of the world. White for white light, the unity of all the colors reflected outward, the growth of spirit and acceptance, and the radiance of protection. The light that uncovers what is hidden. The light that is warm and healing. Green for healing and growth. Yellow because we are a solar-driven world. The sun has the power to heal, soothe, and bring plenty.

OILS AND/OR INCENSES:

Joy and Contentment; Pax/Peace/Osiris; Bountiful Prosperity; Healing; or Peace, Protection, and Blessings.

MEDITATION:

Always thank the god or goddess or whoever helps you with your spiritual work for this beautiful planet and his or her help in preserving it. Ask for guidance about what you can do about saving the planet and helping others to become more aware.

ADDITIONAL SUGGESTIONS:

Recycle. Encourage others to do so also. Perform a ritual daily for the care and continuance of the earth. Tell someone what he or she can do, too; that person may not have thought of it. Use water sparingly. Turn off the faucet when you have wetted your plates or your toothbrush. In some countries it is a day's journey to fetch water. We do not have an endless supply.

Put an image of the world on a green or white cloth on your altar. Cushion it with soft flowers. Make it safe.

❧ THANKS ❧

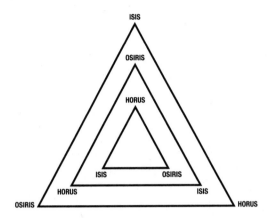

Clearly, giving thanks is the most neglected area of Candle Therapy and psychology. Once a crisis has abated, it is easy to forget to say thank you.

It is very important to acknowledge those who have helped you spiritually. When you have been given blessings, be sure to carve the following symbol on a white or purple candle. This candle is not for getting, just thanking. Buy any flowers for the candle that express your thanks. Candles for thanksgiving promote joy in you, as well as in the spiritual being or friends you are thanking. Below I have used the Egyptian pantheon and trinity. Please feel free to use any religious framework with which you have affinity. Fill in your religious pantheon (God, Jesus, the Holy Ghost, Virgin Mary, all the aspects of Buddha, Allah, Jehovah, Krishna, other Goddesses, etc.) or even your friends who helped you spiritually.

As you go clockwise around the outside to the inside triangles, notice how the names are placed. The name that ends the outer triangle (bottom left corner of each) begins the next smaller triangle at its apex. Isis ends the innermost triangle and is the apex of the outermost one. Continuum is life and our joy.

≈ GIFTS FOR OTHERS ≈

If you cannot decide which symbol is best for you or a friend, use two or three of them. Explain to your friend that he or she should meditate upon the purpose of *each* symbol.

	GIFTS FOR OTHERS
Birthdays	"Happiness and Joy" "Good Fortune and Reversing Bad Luck" "Rebirth" "New Beginnings—Life Changer"
Success	"Success" "Getting a Perfect Job" "Performers, Recognition, Fame, and Connections" "Choose Me"
Marriages	"A Blessing for a Couple"
Anniversaries	"Deepen and Continue a Relationship"
Traveling	"Safe Journeys"
House warming	"House Blessing and Ghost Banishing" "Peace and Harmony"
Healing	"Emotional Healing" "Physical Healing" "Strength" "Stress Reduction" "Weight Loss and Breaking Patterns and Addictions" "A Blast of Sunlight and Energy"

~ THE LAST WORD ~

YOU CAN'T ALWAYS GET WHAT YOU WANT . . .

All prayers are answered; the answer can be yes, no, or maybe. In the words of Oscar Wilde, "When the gods wish to punish us, they answer our prayers." With each candle there is something to be learned, especially if things do not manifest the way you think they should. Try to hear the lesson. When the answer is no, just know that a higher force is probably protecting you from something that is not in your best interest.

I am very grateful for the prayers that were answered with a no. We cannot always know what is right for us. Nonetheless, it's not wrong to ask—it's wrong to *demand.* Have faith that what is best for you will come to you . . . *and it will.*

REMEMBER . . . YOU GET WHAT YOU NEED.

BLESSINGS TO YOU ALL.

APPENDIX

◆

∾ COMPLETE LIST OF MAGICAL OILS AND INCENSES WITH EXPLANATIONS ∾

The following is a list of fragrance blends and essential oils. Any scent can be transformed into an incense in the form of stick, cones, or powder. For more information and a supplier, please visit www.candletherapy.com. The direct e-mail for orders and questions is ordering@candletherapy.com.

Some people avoid using fragrances. Scents, such as Carnation, Lotus, and Lily of the Valley cannot be made into essentials. Fragrance oils may contain other flowers or synthetic scents. Musk and Ambergris, by necessity, must be synthetic. Collecting the essential oil is extremely cruel to animals and is now illegal.

Warning: some oils, such as peppermint or cinnamon, tend to irritate the skin if not diluted in other oils. Please use gloves with these oils, and any other if you are sensitive or pregnant (or planning to be). Don't drink them or put them on any mucous membranes or in the eyes.

Please do not take any of the oils or incenses internally.

Listings *with* * refer to blends. The main scent is listed so you can get a general sense of the predominant smell of the blend. There are other oils beside the main scent blended into these formulae. Listings *without* * are essentials or fragrances.

ACACIA is a floral, sun-oriented oil used for joy, money attraction, psychic development, and altar anointment.

ALLSPICE intensifies whatever work needs a little jolt or extra power. Sparks and initiates ideas. Brings joy, success, money, and luck. Its Mars energy can foster motivation, strength, and confidence. Can also neutralize hurt in relationships and give daily health.

ALMOND brings wisdom and confidence. Gives great energy and alertness. Attracts extravagance and releases inhibitions. Can also attract money.

AMBER does it all. It brings fame, recognition, success, acclaim, happiness, protection, money, and overcomes any obstacles in your way. Good for performers.

AMBERGRIS is exotic oil, which now can be gotten only in its synthetic form, since it comes from whales. Like other smells from animals, such as musk or civet, it is used for sensual attraction. It also is good for relaxation, as well as dream and trance work.

ANISE purifies, rejuvenates, and increases psychic abilities. Can also be used for protection, healing, expansion, joviality, and luck.

*ANGER BE GONE is a zesty rose-based oil, made during the waning moon. It helps one cope with annoyances and let go of pent-up anger and hostile feelings so they are no longer a bother to you. You may be angry for good reasons, so examine what choices you have. Anger sometimes arises from not telling others what you need or not being heard. Put on this oil and empower yourself to express your anger or what you need *in a way that can be heard* and processed to create positive change. Also see Stress Reduction for more help.

*APARTMENT FIND brings the right apartment to you. A very popular city blend.

*APHRODISIAC BLEND (also called Aphrodisiac Potion) inspires lust and passion with its coconut and patchouli essence. Create or enhance an atmosphere of passion with red candles anointed with this blend. Don't, however, use it to manipulate or force someone; it will backfire.

APPLE (also called Apple Blossom) is for peace of mind, relaxation, and successful projects. Brings success, as well as irresistibility and aphrodisiac effects. Attracts friends and lovers.

*ARABKA SOUDAGAR changes bad business luck to good. A great money-drawing blend for businesses.

*ATTRACTION (also called Attract and Find) is a waxing moon mixture of frankincense, myrrh, sandalwood, and a dash of cinnamon can attract and find anything for you—i.e., job, love, friends, money, luck, an apartment, clients, and more.

*ATTRACT SOUL MATE ROMANCE (also called Soul Mate Attraction) has a peachy scent that attracts the highest love to you. Envision and make lists of the qualities you would like your mate to possess. Wear daily or when socializing. Concentrate upon attracting that special someone. Use when you are ready to meet a long-term mate.

BALM OF GILEAD heals a broken heart and brings awareness of the radiance of inner self. Also, eases the pain of loss. Protects and calms. Not only does it help one to let go of past love, but it also brings new love. A very sensual oil.

*BANISHING removes all negativity, bad influences, spirits, and even lingering roommates and relatives with the power of bay and rose.

BASIL draws money, cleanses, and blesses the home. It also brings positive energy, happiness, mental stimulation, and prosperity. It creates harmony. Apply before an anticipated disagreement between you and another. Put drops of Basil into an unscented blending oil because it can be irritating to the skin in pure oil form.

*BAST brings joy and appreciation of the precious little things in life, like a reflection in a cup of tea or being bundled up in front of a fire on a rainy day.

BAY uncrosses, removes negativity, and protects. With sun power, it draws money, wealth, and success. It harmonizes opposite qualities and gives strength. Brings visions and insight.

BAYBERRY is used to bring prosperity, wealth, blessings, and plenty. That is why it is associated with new beginnings and giving at Yule and Christmas.

BENZOIN (related to and can be a substitute for Storax) is a resin used for strong protection and purification. Can be used to send your thoughts and prayers to loved ones who have died. According to *Cunningham's Encyclopedia of Magical Herbs,* a mixture of benzoin, cinnamon, and basil can attract success and customers. It improves mental abilities and removes obstacles. Also brings a sense of personal power, as well as peace of mind and freedom from outside worries.

BERGAMOT is the beautiful and expensive scent used in Earl Grey tea. It heals, fights depression, brings sun energy, and instills joy. Brings confidence, success, and power to overcome obstacles. Protects, attracts riches, and leads to new opportunities.

*BLESSED LIGHT AND THANKS is for giving thanks and acknowledging the gifts you have you received.

*BLESSING (also called Altar) has a calming lavender scent and is excellent for blessing objects and bringing blessings into one's life. Also good for thanking the gods and goddesses.

*BLISS is made during the full moon and is an uplifting carnation-based blend that brings exquisite bliss and joy! Great for beating the blues!

*BOUNTIFUL PROSPERITY (also called Prosperity) is a fruity blend made during the waxing moon for bringing great plenty in all areas of life.

CALAMUS is used in many spiritual formulae. It psychically clears, cleanses, and attracts the highest energies. It also heals, protects, strengthens spells, and attracts love. When the herb is sprinkled in the corners of your kitchen, it banishes poverty.

*CALL ME does just what it says! It gets someone to call for business or pleasure. Anoint the phone or a candle with this hyacinth-based oil or light the incense and envision the person calling. Don't be alarmed if the phone rings while you're meditating on this!

CAMELLIA is great for personal growth and a heightened sense of self and confidence. When added to Venus oil, it heightens the appreciation and awareness of one's womanhood.

CAMPHOR is a natural for uncrossing and purification. Used in many traditional cold remedies. It also brings purity and celibacy.

CARDAMON attracts love and gives a sexy spice to situations.

CARNATION rejuvenates and energizes but, simultaneously, soothes and calms. It refreshes the body and renews the emotions. Aids in healing and removing negativity. Very strong protection.

CEDAR (also called Cedarwood) is very grounding and cleansing. Protects the home against evil and damage. Eliminates nightmares. Very empowering and spiritually uplifting. Also used in money blends to attract wealth and security.

CHAMOMILE is very, very, very relaxing. Throw it into a bath and slide back into peaceful meditation. It is also good for purification and unhexing.

CHERRY brings joy, confidence, humor, and life. Gets rid of worries.

CINNAMON attracts wealth, prosperity, and success. It is good for calming, concentration, psychic awareness, healing, and protection. Great for balancing and adding a dash of passion to a situation. Very irritating to the skin. At most, use one drop in any oil blends you wear.

CIVET is a synthetic oil that is used in musky blends for lusty attraction. It originally came from cats' testicles. Use only one drop or it will overpower any oil blend. It smells really foul by itself!

*CLARITY (also called Test Taking and Concentration) helps the seeker see clearly and understand the issues at hand. Take a deep sniff to gain insight. Increases focus, mental clarity, and concentration. Great for making decisions. Put the oil on your third eye for clarity in all situations.

*CLEOPATRA is one of the most powerful ancient formulae for attraction, seduction, and excitement. It combines the flavors of Balm of Gilead and orange to seduce everyone!

CLOVE gives comfort to the bereaved. Also good for inspiration, memory, protection, inner strength, courage, and healing. It also stops gossip and keeps away negativity. Can be irritating to the skin.

COCONUT heals, breaks spells, and protects home and property. Also brings chastity.

*COME TO ME does what it says and is pushy about it. Could border on manipulation if used incorrectly. Best used as an attraction blend for meeting new people.

*COMPLETION finalizes whatever is outstanding. It brings negotiations to a close. Good for decision and deal making.

*CONQUERING GLORY is a spicy dragon's blood blend with a dash of cinnamon. To assure its power, it is made during the waning moon to overcome whatever obstacles are in the way to your success. Great for being chosen at job interviews and auditions. You will conquer with glory.

COPAL is a tree resin usually from South America used for high spirituality, purification, and protection. Good for blessing temples and homes.

*COPING (also called Versatile) brings the ability to deal with the situations at hand and whatever is thrown at you—even the overwhelming ones. This rose-based essence brings flexibility and peace.

CORIANDER is good for general healing. Stimulates the mind.

*COURTING attracts people to court you or changes what you have into a courting situation. Can attract interest in you that could lead to a serious relationship.

*CROWN OF SUCCESS overcomes whatever is in your way to achieving your highest success. This orris- and vetivert-based oil is different from Conquering Glory, because it should be saved for your *greatest* success. Use Conquering Glory for all other obstacle removing.

CUCUMBER is used to instill fertility and healing. Gets rid of headaches.

CYCLAMEN is for safe passage and all kinds of transitions—even protected sleep. Good for childbirth, life passages, and all kinds of new beginnings without grief or remorse.

CYPRESS is excellent for consecration, healing, longevity, and protection. Good for reaching the dead or acknowledging the dark of the moon. Gives an easy passage for a loved one who has just died. Eases grief, worry, loss, and ends arguments, especially between mothers and children.

DAMIANA taps into Mars and sun emergies to be a powerful aphrodisiac. Use as an oil, incense, or tea. Please consult an herbal guide, herbalist, or physician before taking any herb internally for interactions, proper usage, and its appropriateness for you.

DEER'S-TONGUE was named because it looks like the tongue of a deer. Like Damiana, it awakens lust and is a strong attraction herb. In oil form, it has a sweet earthy scent, which can overcome impotence.

*DIXIE LOVE is an old Southern blend that makes you irresistible. Works on people from all parts of the country (and the world).

DRAGON'S BLOOD is an herb that, when dried, is red—like blood. It is a strong protector. It empowers and quiets. Scott Cunningham, in his *Encyclopedia of Magical Herbs,* suggests you can quiet a noisy household by mixing the powder with salt in a bottle, covering it tightly, and hiding it in a secret place in your home.

*EARTH is a patchouli-based scent for grounding and centering. Also good as a devotional to Mother Earth.

*EGYPTIAN TEMPLE brings forth the dry and sweet lotus-filled winds of the temple and a peaceful environment to create a sacred space around your home or altar.

EUCALYPTUS is the scent in all steam rooms. It heals, revitalizes, rejuvenates, protects, and stimulates. A sacred scent of purification, enlightenment, and recuperation. Traditional remedies for colds, sore throats, and respiratory disorders contain eucalyptus.

*EVERYTHING is a fruity blend of everything! It has love, money, protection, clarity, wishing, joy . . . you name it. It is important, when using this oil, to concentrate on what "everything" is for you every time you wear it.

*FAITH is a relaxing gardenia blend to bring the strength to have faith. Boosts confidence and makes it possible to be optimistic, keep trying, and know the best thing will happen.

*FEARLESSNESS AND CONFIDENCE is the perfect oil for conquering fears and insecurities. It is also very potent for courage and pushing projects forward. The frankincense and vanilla in this blend gives it extra strength.

*FIERY WALL OF PROTECTION creates a solid wall through which nothing can pierce. Protects from evil and harm. Take practical and reality-based precautions as well.

*FLYING is a patchouli blend that makes your psyche fly to another level. Good for freeform meditations, astral travel, and merging with the ethers. Perfect Halloween blend. Based on the ancient formula, but without the hallucinatory (and illegal) ingredients.

FRANGIPANI (also called Plumeria) grows all over Hawaii and is the main flower in the leis. For centuries, it has been one of the classic scents in French perfumers' love blends. It fosters joie de vivre, love, trust, and friendships. Flirty.

FRANKINCENSE brings in the blessings of the sun, especially after purifying with myrrh. Fosters wealth, health, confidence, fearlessness, success, acclaim, spiritual awakening, and mental clarity. Removes mental blocks. It also can be a purifier. Use it for exorcism, consecration, and protection. May be irritating to the skin.

GALANGAL (also known as Low John or Chewing John) overcomes obstacles and draws money. Carry the root or wear the oil if you need luck in court.

GARDENIA is a classic marriage and true-love flower. It strengthens commitments. Increases the sense of knowing another and harmony. Protects love. Also helps healing and brings peace.

GINGER A spicy and stimulating oil/herb used to attract love, money, courage, and sex. According to *The Herb Book*, by John Lust, the root increases the appetite (for lots of things, it seems).

*GLAMOUR AND SEDUCTION makes one fabulous and alluring with a full moon blast of ambergris and musk. Inspires sexual pleasures. Very passionate, but may not always be the highest person for you. If looking for true love, apply Long-Lasting Love (or a similar blend) at the same time.

*GLITZ, FUN, AND LUST is one of our most popular blends. We thought it was just because our store was in New York City. Boy, were we wrong. Seems like this is a popular concept throughout the world. It's spicy and buttery and delicious. Very lusty, very fun, very glittery. Have fun!

*GOONA GOONA mixes patchouli and rose to foster trust, communication, and understanding. This is a wonderful oil to ease relationship problems.

*GRIEVING AND COMFORT's ingredients are gently combined to ease the pain of losing a loved one. This soothing lotus-based compound heals the heart. Helps mourning and healing.

*HAS NO HANNA eliminates depression and poverty. This formula includes an open safety pin in the bottle to spiritually hook prosperity and plenty.

HAZEL (also called Hazelwood) gives wisdom and fertility. Carry a hazelnut to further increase fertility. You can also use a hazel twig to draw a protective circle around yourself and to make an excellent magical wand.

*HEALING (also called Health) is an intensive gardenia essence that helps attune one to vibrations to heal the body and mind. Also helps enhance, preserve, maintain, or gain health.

HEATHER is protective from violence, especially that directed toward women. It brings love as would be given by a child. Therefore, it can stop the passion of a relationship and bring it back to a joyous friendship. Wonderful for blessing a home and having good dreams.

HELIOTROPE was named for the Egyptian city of Helios, which was the center for worship of the Sun God. The power of the sun brings light, great wealth, and blessings. It can uncover through knowledge and prophetic dreams.

*HIGHEST OPPORTUNITIES AND OPEN DOORS does just that! Amazing success blend. Same as Mercury oil.

HIGH JOHN THE CONQUEROR comes from the jalup root. Used for conquering and overcoming obstacles, and being chosen over the competition. Brings victory, wealth, success, wishes, travel, and acclaim.

*HIGH PRIESTESS brings forth mysteries that have not been revealed. Sends seeker to higher level of awareness.

HONEYSUCKLE can be used for a final exam or even writing a perfect love letter. It heightens the mind and memory. It also brings eloquence in writing and verbal expression. Also attracts cash and good luck.

*HOUSE BLESSING can be used alone or after a good smudging with sage. For blessing and cleansing a new home or spiritually clearing an old one.

HYACINTH is good for relaxing and easing the pain of childbirth. Also relieves grief and nightmares. Eases obsessions and depression.

HYSSOP is a very strong protection and uncrossing herb. Can cleanse from mental sadness and guilt.

*INDIAN BOUQUET brings harmony to warring couples. Brings peace and understanding.

*INSPIRATION AND CREATIVITY is a waxing moon blend, which sings with violet and brings incredible creativity and inspiration. Overcomes creative blocks in a big way! Burn the incense when creating a masterwork or getting rid of the blocks to do so.

*IRIS PERFUME increases determination, concentration, and will.

*IRRESISTIBILITY makes you irresistible and tasty smelling. Can be used for business or pleasure. It's good to throw a dash into any endeavor.

*ISIS is a beautiful heather-based oil created for the Egyptian goddess of love, rebirth, and creation. Orange and myrrh oils transport you to her throne. Bring yourself in touch with the energy, high mysteries, and wisdom of Isis.

JALAP See High John the Conqueror.

JASMINE is both sensual and spiritual. It calms, helps sleep, and imagination. It clears negative memories and worries. Sensually, it can attract love and sexual encounters. Spiritually, it is a wonderful meditation scent, which induces deep trance and high insight.

*JOY AND CONTENTMENT is a waxing moon blend of sweet florals such as acacia. This concoction injects the daily jolt of empowerment and joy you need. For banishing depression.

JUNIPER is a great protection against everything from accidents to ghosts. Gets rid of negativity and lack of clarity. Heals and purifies. Brings luck and blessings.

*JUPITER inspires justice, fairness, mercy, expansion, vision, and truth. Can be used for winning court cases and gaining a judge's mercy.

*KHUS KHUS is an old Southern blend to cause you to be irresistible to the opposite sex.

*KINDLY SPIRIT makes people like you and be sympathetic to your cause. Especially useful for court cases.

*KYPHI is a sultry scent for not only healing but also banishing negativity.

LAVENDER is a wonderful antidepression, calming, and sleep-inducing scent. It is also used for clearing the mind and bringing health and vitality. Brings true and respectful love.

LEMON is used in most healing, uncrossing, and protection formulae. Also, and importantly, it cleanses. Why do you think grocery store cleansers are lemon-scented? Lilac and lavender, traditionally, have also been spiritual cleansers. This was reflected in the marketplace. We have now generally forgotten the roots of this fragrance choice. Lemon washes any negative vibrations off of magical pieces if they have been in some way corrupted.

LEMONGRASS, LEMON VERBENA See Verbena.

*LETTING GO helps you to let go gently and completely. Good for uncrossing and bringing in new love. Let go of the old; bring in the new.

LILAC, like Lemon, has been chosen as a cleanser scent to this day. Lilac purifies and removes evil. Cleanses hauntings, too. It brings peace and harmony, as well as improved decision-making ability and memory. Attracts fun love—maybe not forever, though.

LILY protects against evil and unwanted guests. Brings strength and insight. In *Cunningham's Encyclopedia of Magical Herbs,* Scott Cunningham states that the way to solve a recent crime is to bury an old piece of leather in a lily bed.

LILY OF THE VALLEY is poisonous for internal use. The flowers are often combined with red roses in wedding bouquets to represent the merging of purity and passion. In order to achieve, we need the balance of a great passion with the control to accomplish it. For example, you cannot, as an actor, be drunk while playing a drunk. This flower and scent brings serenity, peace, confidence, happiness, and mental strength.

LIME makes up many commercial attraction scents and aftershaves. It can release inhibitions and attract the best love to you. Very sexual and intense, too. Also is a strong protector against evil.

*LINGERING LOVE is a romantic gardenia-based oil that keeps you on the mind of your loved one. This is the idea upon which the entire perfume industry is based. This is the magical blend they wish they had!

*LONG-LASTING LOVE attracts love for potential long-term relationships. Its beautiful rose and frangipani scent attracts a pure, soul mate level love.

LOTUS gives gifts of healing, spirituality, protection, and insights from the spirits. Used for a dressing and altar oil, as well as a healing oil. Converts mood and thoughts from sad to glad. Clears and uncrosses. Good meditative scent and a symbol of long life in the East. A sacred offering and spiritual symbol in Egypt.

*LOVE CLARITY brings clarity to you about relationships.

*LOVE DEEPENING is a jasmine-based oil that deepens your ongoing relationship. Takes your relationship to the next level. Be sure not to be impatient and force it! Sometimes the next level and deepening takes time. Sometimes you might need Goona Goona (for trust) or Mercury (for communication) instead of this. Analyze what is the specific problem at hand and try to choose the scent that best addresses it.

*LOVE HEALING is for sweetly healing a relationship with many oils such as pine and rose. This is essential for people trying to reunite a lost love. You must heal whatever keeps you apart before you can be back together again.

*LOVE INTOXICATION is a sexy, intoxicating strawberry blend that bends the heart of whomever you focus upon. Great for enhancing attraction and sprucing up your current love relationship.

LOVE OPENNESS opens you and another up to love. Be careful not to force another to be open or to love you. Explore other choices, such as Goona Goona or Sun, if openness is defined by your wishes.

*LOVE POTION 131 is the love oil you need it to be. It is the most flexible love attraction blend. It brings the best love to you. Rose and lily help attract the best love to you, for this time in your life. This is the perfect oil if you want love and just are not sure if it should be serious, transition, or a fling.

*LOVE PROTECTION protects the love you have from external forces.

*LOVE UNCROSSING removes whatever negativity or outside influences could be keeping you and a lover apart. (Not for removing lovers who might be distracting your mate, but it will take away the problems and disagreements between you two so you can reunite). Also good to use between relationships to erase any lingering negative influences of past love.

*LUCKY HAND brings luck. It is based on the tale of the monkey's paw. Be careful of what you pray for! You could get it.

*LUCKY JOB finds the perfect job for you! Meditate upon what the perfect job entails. Make lists and carry a High John the Conqueror root to the interview. Good luck!

*LUCKY LODESTONE (also called Magnet) attracts luck to a project and changes bad luck to good.

*LUCKY SEVEN ROOT protects against being hexed by unknown enemies.

*MAGNET See Lucky Lodestone.

MAGNOLIA brings someone to you and keeps them faithful. Good for finding lost items. It's also good for meditation and psychic work. Protects against psychic attacks.

MARJORAM keeps loyalty and security around you. Calming and rejuvenating. Overcomes depression and strengthens love.

*MARS AND MOTIVATION gets you moving and motivated with its pungent rosemary and peppercorns. Eliminates procrastination. Gives energy and fearlessness to any pursuit. It also gets you in touch with the energy, fire, power, and passion of Mars. Use with caution. Not advised for situations where anger is a problem.

*MASTER is used to master a situation and gain control. Great for addictions and overeating. The main ingredient, patchouli, is great for hunger reduction and mastering your own will (in any other issue). Never use it to master anyone else's will—if you do you will be obsessed or controlled in some way three times worse.

*MERCURY enhances communication and opens the doors to connections, opportunities, and smooth dealings. Also enhances concentration and inspiration. Besides possessing the power of the planet, this oil can bring the aid of the mythical winged messenger Mercury to speed up tasks and ensure safe journeys. This does not contain the deadly quicksilver found in thermometers.

MIMOSA protects you from negative dreams and energies. Baths in mimosa unhex. Place a sprig under your pillow for bringing out dreams and subconscious desires.

MINT Not only is it great in mint juleps and iced tea, mint has tremendous healing and protective abilities. It attracts good spirits and stimulates lusty feelings. Put a few leaves in your wallet for attracting money.

MISTLETOE is symbolically associated with fertility, since mistletoe bears berries when winter has taken all the other fruit. The medical foundation of this association with libido is that mistletoe has a high concentration of progesterone, among other sterols.

*MONEY (also called Money Drawing) is used to bring money from all possible sources. It's amazing, but this sunny blend actually smells like money. Concentrate on the minimum amount you need and inscribe it on a candle or meditate upon the figure as you anoint yourself with the oil. You can add that you would appreciate receiving more cash, but you would be grateful for whatever is your "minimum to survive" amount. Be sure to concentrate on gathering your money from the best and legal sources.

*MOON is a wonderful floral-based blend for healing and worshipping the moon goddess. It is a soulful meditation blend as well.

MUSK comes from deer in its natural form. Therefore, our only forms are synthetic and are made to emulate the musky deer pheromones. Humans seem to respond to the pheromones, making this one of the most popular ingredients in sex blends. Also gives willpower and determination.

MYRRH was used in the temples of Ra and Isis in Egypt. It purifies space and consecrates objects. Fosters high spiritual awakening and uplifting. It is good for getting justice for your cause (for example, winning in court), but you better make doubly sure that you are totally innocent. Justice *will* be served. So if you are guilty, Myrrh will judge you, too.

MYRTLE promotes love and fidelity. Keeps love alive and exciting. Worn by brides to prevent rapid pregnancy. Yet, also is an herb that promotes fertility when it's time. Brings youthfulness and money.

*MYSTERIOUS makes you alluring and mysterious with a combination of patchouli and jasmine to light up the night—and make your day.

*MYSTIC SEER (also called Mystic Seeker or Wisdom) is a lotus and sandalwood mixture that can be worn on your third eye to open awareness and induce prophetic visions. Concentrate upon finding wisdom and opening the inner doors to light.

NARCISSUS gives confidence, strength, fearlessness, and will. Great for the shy. Can make you the life of the party! In the party of life! Induces self-love.

NEROLI is orange blossom. This is a classic love, as well as wealth-attraction, scent. The sun aspect adds life, joy, fame, purification, and obstacle removal. Wonderful for alleviating sleep disturbances.

*NEW BEGINNINGS is fresh, sweet, and pine-based. It brings about new life and starts in either all or specific areas of life. Also makes transitions smooth. Great for starting again.

NUTMEG brings the expansion of Jupiter. It enhances concentration, mind power, and studying. Nutmeg can foster trust, understanding, luck, and protection. If you feel negativity and/or curses are coming your way, anoint an egg with nutmeg oil (or fill a small coffinlike box with the powder) and bury it far away from your house. The negativity will be buried along with the egg or box.

OAKMOSS attracts money. Rub it or a money-drawing oil onto four corners of any size currency. Envision attracting more of the same. Put it in your wallet. Be sure not to spend that one bill.

ORANGE is a solar scent, classic for courting and love. It is used in fertility and marriage celebrations because an orange tree is one of the only trees to have fruit and flowers simultaneously. Since it is a symbol of both virginity and fertility, brides sometimes carry it. Orange brings the feeling of courting and respect to the relationship. It is purifying, comforting, calming, and soothing, too. Oranges are also bringers of good luck and fortune. According to *Cunningham's Encyclopedia of Magical Herbs,* if you want a question answered, count the seeds in an orange that you are eating. An even number means no and an odd means yes.

ORRIS is used for attracting success, deep love, and commitment. As a success root or oil, it is good for drawing money and success to you. It is another marriage-oriented scent because it is sacred to *both* Isis and Osiris. Carry an Orris root to attract your true long-lasting love.

PATCHOULI is good for earthly matters and balancing. This oil is great for lust, money, power, as well as fertility and grounding. Enhances animal magnetism and the workings of nature. Good for finalizing business deals (because it is sacred to both Saturn and the sun) and mastering your own will.

*PAX/PEACE/OSIRIS creates a positive, peaceful atmosphere around the wearer, even when chaotic.

*PEACE, PROTECTION, AND BLESSINGS brings all three! This mixes heather, lemon, and peppermint (among other things) to form a powerful shield of light.

PEACH creates respect and decorum in any situation. Good to add to love and work blends. Attracts love fertility. Good for inducing wisdom in the wearer to have the clarity to choose for his or her highest good.

PEPPERMINT revitalizes and refreshes. Peps you up. Uncrosses and attracts good luck. Lifts one's spirit and can bring prophetic dreams. Brings clarity and motivation. It can be irritating to the skin in oil form.

*PERFORMERS AND FAME brings success, fame, skill, confidence, recognition, money, and connections. This amber-based blend is a favorite of writers, musicians, and actors.

PINE gets rid of negativity and is another scent chosen for cleansers—for very spiritual reasons. With Mars's power, Pine creates new starts, cleanses the old, and removes creative blocks. Pine needles can purify a home, when burned, or exorcise evil when scattered on the floor. Also attracts blessings such as money, safety, and healing. Pinecones are old symbols of fertility and increase, if carried.

*PROTECTION brings protection and security. See also Peace, Protection, and Blessings.

*PURIFICATION AND REJUVENATION purifies and brings new life with anise, almond, and other herbs. Smells like cookies from childhood. Cleanses bad memories from the past.

*QUEEN is used by women to attract men for passion.

REBIRTH AND REJUVENATION brings a new you and a complete new beginning in the areas you need. Especially powerful for internal growth. Boost self-esteem, energy, and confidence with florals and sweet freesia.

ROSE is the most classic scent and flower of love and devotion. Most love oils will contain Rose in the blend. It also enhances sex, beauty, and peace. It's also calming and washes away negativity. Red and white roses represent the dual nature (passion and purity) of the goddess Venus.

ROSE GERANIUM is used as a powerful uncrossing and protecting agent. Uncrosses, removes negativity, burdens, and worries. It brings blessings, protection, love, and courage. High spiritual vibration.

ROSEMARY is good for easing labor in childbirth. Don't take internally, please. Also sends away bad vibes, illness, nightmares, headaches, and even old age. Generally gives a sense of strength, being loved, and well-being. Gives centered energy and motivation. When burned, it can produce the answers to unsolved problems.

RUE is a very strong protector from evil and curses. Removes curses, negativity, and jealousy within. Can help one to let go of unrequited love.

SAGE cleanses and purges people, places, and things. Burn a smudge of sage and walk counterclockwise around your room or home to remove negativity and bad spirits. Helps induce sleep and trancework by calming and centering the mind. Ensures longevity, promotes wisdom, and attracts money.

*SAINT JUDE can be called upon when anything you are endeavoring seems impossible. He is the patron saint of impossible causes. Be sure to show your gratitude and sing his praises. Use only after you have tried everything else.

SANDALWOOD is an exotic wood that may become more endangered at some point, so use with respect. There was an importing ban for a while that may return because of the depletion of the trees. Sandalwood oil and incense is the all-time, all-purpose spiritual oil/incense. It aids in all spiritual work, as well as granting wisdom, creativity, and sensual stimulation.

*SAN RAMON attracts customers and sales to your business.

*SATURN finalizes negotiations in business or finances. Brings wisdom and strength. Gives you insight into all the loopholes and angles. Also good for centering, grounding, reducing chaos, and making serious decisions.

*SEVEN AFRICAN POWERS originated in the religious practices of Santeria. The seven powers are the strengths of the seven "Orishas" or gods. For non-Santeria practitioners, this is a powerful blend of vanilla and rose among other things, which empower individuals in seven personal areas of their lives. Make a list of the seven areas, such as love, success, peace, etc., or seven ways to resolve an issue.

*SHI SHI attracts money fast. Eliminates poverty and draws cash.

SPIKENARD brings stability and fidelity to a relationship or situation. (Remember not to manipulate another's will.) Brings fond memories, one's higher self, guardian spirits, and health.

*SPIRITUAL SEX is used for experiencing sex on a spiritual level (with and without a partner). It seems to work best when you already are sexually involved in a trusting love relationship. The ambergris-scented oil helps make the sexual experience more spiritual and intimate. Out-of-this-world intimacy!

STRAWBERRY is powerfully sexual, lusty, and passionate. Just envision the chocolate-covered strawberries. Magnetic and intoxicating.

*STRESS REDUCTION reduces stress, tension, bad vibes, and fighting. Take a whiff of this floral and citrus blend anytime you need to calm yourself. Enables user to concentrate and focus.

STRONG PROTECTION is the most powerful protection blend. Use for the most dire circumstances.

*SUCCESS (also called Solid Success) is a serious all-purpose blend with orris predominating. A waxing moon blend that is great for propelling business ventures and building careers. Brings stable success in whatever areas need it.

*SUCCESS BLAST yields a serious blast of success. It gets careers and projects moving. Give your success a blast of sunshine.

*SUN has two aspects, the deep and the bright. Therefore Deep Sun is a spicy frankincense and myrrh essence and Sunny Sun is uplifting citrus. Either blend bathes the wearer in the joy and warmth of the sun. It does everything. It can bring health, wealth, happiness, fame, and success. It also brings the healing and restorative powers of the sun. The sun brings the hidden to light and makes one noticed. Others will be attracted to your radiance. Good for Leos, too, as their planetary scent. This oil also imbues the wearer with recognition and fame.

*SUPER FAST LUCK (also called Fast Luck or Good Luck.) brings fast luck to any endeavor with a spicy mix of patchouli and rose. The waxing moon doubles the punch of this rapid-acting oil. Also reverses bad luck.

*SWEET MAGICAL TRANCE is so calming; it can feel like a sweet trance. Good for visions, astral travel, and prophetic dreams. This floral scent is also for making your magical workings sweet. Clears obstacles to higher truths.

THYME brings irresistibility, courage, and compassion. Protects from others' negative thoughts and actions. Commonly used for purification and health spells. Stimulates action.

TONKA surrounds one with positive feelings, luck, and wealth. Reverses bad feelings. It turns enemies into friends. Attracts love and grants wishes.

TUBEROSE relaxes and sends peace. Attracts secure and peaceful love relationships.

*UNCROSSING (also called Clearing) unhexes and eliminates all negativity and bad vibrations with lemon, bay, rose, and more.

VANILLA is good for a little of everything. It's a split audience. Half the people wear it to be alluring and fabulous. The other half uses it for successful business dealings and luck. Also gives strength, energy, and power. Brings feelings of joy, openness, and freedom.

*VAVOOM is for big-time sex appeal and flair. Be the most *faaabulous* you can be!

*VENUS is not only a devotional blend for the goddess Venus, but also a classic rose-based love scent for love that lasts. It is also an oil that draws the beauty and attraction of Venus. Attracts beauty, love, friendship, and money.

VERBENA (also called Lemon Verbena) is a lemongrass for healing and cleansing. Good as a purification bath. This Mercury-oriented scent/herb opens and speeds mental abilities and psychic awareness. Calms you so you can find the beginning point of an overwhelming task. Then helps you reasonably pace any activity for the greatest success. Also can be used for love blends to enhance attractiveness.

VERVAIN protects you and your home, especially from storms. (Please supplement with earthly efforts to protect your home!) Vervain in your home or garden attracts wealth and success. Brings eternal youth and no disturbing dreams. A great herb/oil/incense to bring forth creativity (especially in the written and verbal word) and success in artistic pursuits. A favorite of performers.

VETIVERT grounds and unhexes in a big way. Just a drop can make you more balanced, tolerant, and protected from all harm. Put it on your cash register to attract money and prevent robberies.

VIOLET is a love scent that brings high respect and depth. It lends emotional comfort and aids in straightening out estrangements. Helps wishes come true. Brings peace, healing, and sleep. Protects against spirits.

*VOODOO NIGHTS SEX is luscious and sexy. Use this lime-based oil to attract a lover, enhance your love life, and to experience the ultimate in sex (especially with a loved one).

WATERMELON is associated with fertility, pregnancy, and plenty. A great seduction oil, too.

*WISH FULFILLMENT (also called Mojo Wishing or Wishing) grants power, favors, and that special wish. Use other oils and incenses that are more specific first, in order to develop your wish. If you are wishing for the perfect love, use Attract Soul Mate Romance or Love Potion 131. If you are waiting for the perfect job, you might use Super Fast Luck or Attraction. If you are *very, very* clear use this oil and make a wish on a star. Be careful; you might get what you wish for! Be prepared and make sure it's for the highest good of all involved. Mojo rising!

WINTERGREEN brings healing, good fortune, and success in exams and tests. Removes hexes. Attracts good spirits to your magical requests and workings.

WISTERIA helps you pass a test or some mental challenge with ease. It also brings blessings, positive feelings, and higher spiritual awareness.

WORMWOOD is the ingredient in the addictive drink absinthe. Wormwood is still intoxicating us today magically. It opens the mind to psychic awareness, dreams, and mysteries of the dark moon.

YLANG YLANG is an expensive floral scent for luck, finding good employment, and making decisions. Makes one attractive, impressive, and expressive.

BIBLIOGRAPHY

◆

Cunningham, Scott. *Cunningham's Encyclopedia of Magical Herbs,* 2nd edition. St. Paul: Llewellyn Publications, 1985.

Cunningham, Scott. *The Magical Household.* St. Paul: Llewellyn Publications, 1987.

Farrar, Janet and Stewart. *Spells and How They Work.* Custer, Washington: Farrar, Phoenix Publishing, 1990.

Lust, John. *The Herb Book.* New York: Bantam Books, 1974.

ABOUT THE AUTHOR

◆

Dr. Catherine Riggs-Bergesen is a licensed clinical psychologist in New York City. She also owns Other Worldly Waxes and Whatever, which is dedicated to the principles of this book. She, her magical candles, and stores have appeared on numerous broadcasts, such as: *The Joan Rivers Show, National Geographic Explorer, NBC Nightly News, Real Personal, Today, Fox News, Good Day New York, MTV House of Style, Religion & Ethics*, news programs in Finland and Italy, and WABC-AM radio.

Publications in which she has been featured include the *New York Times*; the *New York Post*; the *New York Daily News*; the *New York Press*; *New Woman*; publications linked to the Reuters wire service; CNN on the Web; *Nikki Woman* (Japan); *Harper's Bazaar*; *Colors* (Benetton's magazine); *Elle* (Italy); *Paper*; *US FrontLine*; *Time Out New York*; *Gerry Frank's Where to Find It, Buy It, Eat It in New York*; *The Village Voice* . . . and more.

All questions, comments, mail orders, and suggestions are welcome. For correspondence:
Dr. Catherine Riggs-Bergesen
Candle Therapy
Madison Square Station
P.O. Box 1540
New York, New York 10159-1540
catherine@candletherapy.com